REMEMBER HER FOR THIS

A Study on the Women in the Gospels

REMEMBER HER FOR THIS

A Study on the Women in the Gospels

Deborah Kaine
THOMPSON

Initials in parenthesis after scripture references indicate different translations of the Bible. All scripture quotations, unless otherwise indicated, are taken from the *Holy Bible, New International Version®*, NIV®. Copyright ©1973, 1978, 1984, 2011 by Biblica, Inc.™ Used by permission of Zondervan. All rights reserved worldwide. www.zondervan.com The "NIV" and "New International Version" are trademarks registered in the United States Patent and Trademark Office by Biblica, Inc.™

Some scripture verses are from *The Message* and are marked as such. Copyright © 1993, 1994, 1995, 1996, 2000, 2001, 2002. Used by Permission of NavPress, All Rights Reserved. www.navpress.com.

Scripture verses marked TLB are taken from *The Living Bible* copyright © 1971 by Tyndale House Foundation. Used by permission of Tyndale House Publishers Inc., Carol Stream, Illinois 60188. All rights reserved.

Scripture verses marked KJV are taken from the *King James Version of the Bible.*

Remember Her For This: A Study on Women in the Gospels is published by:
E-maginative Writing, Mesa, AZ 85209

First released in 2013 in electronic format under the title:
Face-to-Face: The Women Who Met Jesus

For information on this or other books by Deborah Kaine Thompson, please direct emails to: kaine@e-maginativewriting.com

Visit our website: e-maginativewriting.com

Printed in the United States of America

ISBN: 978-0-9856956-7-5

Dedicated
to my
mother
sister
aunts
nieces
grandmothers
daughters-in-law
mothers-in-law
granddaughters
and girlfriends
and to the
One
who
freed
us all

ACKNOWLEDGMENTS

There are a few people I must thank who stood by me and helped me through the long process of researching and writing this book. They believed that God had put this message on my heart and urged me to finish it and bring it to a wider audience.

I want to thank my readers Debbie Williams, Jean Boyd, and Bev Hjermstad whose gentle criticism and enthusiastic praise were deeply appreciated. I want to give a special acknowledgment to Paula White for being an excellent sounding board as I shared my "downloads" with her. She inspired me to trust the Lord in the process.

I am deeply grateful for the spiritual guidance, biblical knowledge, and intellectual input of my pastors Al and Carole Venditti. They are a living example of humble service to the Lord and their impact on the Body of Christ cannot be measured.

I want to thank my editor Jeanne Feeney who polished my manuscript and challenged my perspective, bringing greater clarity to the work. I also want to thank my sister Rebekah Ballmer and my mother June Kirn who gave me their encouragement and valuable opinions.

Most importantly, I want to thank Jesus, my Lord and Savior, who urged me through *Shekinah* to "free the women" by bringing a new feminine perspective to the Gospels. Many times I marveled at and was humbled by the insights I received. I am grateful to God that he first loved me — just as I am.

CONTENTS

"And I tell you this in solemn truth,
that wherever the Good News is preached throughout the world,
this woman's deed will be remembered and praised."

Mark 14:9 (TLB)

INTRODUCTION

This book is the compilation of years of study and research on how women can reach their full potential in the modern Christian church. I have sought to bring a feminine perspective to these age-old stories, repeatedly told and interpreted by popes, priests, pastors, and kings — all of whom were male. I do not present myself as a theologian or a feminist scholar but as a devout Christian who has walked the path for more than forty years.

The aim of this book is to provide a new understanding of Jesus and to reveal the ways he viewed and interacted with women. I have included meditations and study guide questions in every chapter. Readers will also find a blank page to write notes, comments, or answers to the questions at the end of each chapter. It is helpful to examine these women's face-to-face encounters with Jesus. He is our model, the head of our church. We can have no better example.

You will be pleased that these accounts from the Gospels confirm that Jesus was known to appreciate women. He values them. He listens to them. He empathizes with them. He empowers them. He elevates them. During his earthly ministry, he would stop whatever he was doing in order to spend time with them. He took every opportunity to free them, not only from sin, illness, and death but also from societal, legal, and religious oppression. He revealed the character and heart of God to these women, intending for these encounters to be remembered and included in his Word.

These women's stories continue to be told because divine truth was imparted in them. When you consider these unique encounters, you will realize God wants his daughters to share the fullness of his Spirit. Jesus came so all people might have life and have it in abundance.

About a year ago, I was deep in prayer when *Shekinah*[1] (the Holy Spirit) spoke into my heart three words: "Free the women." I did not know what this could mean for my life. I devoted myself to praying, meditating, and researching what this seemingly simple request could signify. Did it mean to literally free innocent women from the world's prisons? Did it call me to become involved with eradicating sex trafficking? How about the women virtually imprisoned in their homes, fearing domestic violence?

While all these crimes against women are horrifying, I felt such paths of action were not meant for me. I sought further guidance from the Lord. I knew the message I had received came from the divine presence of Shekinah because the words gripped my spirit and mind. I could not stop wrestling with the intent of those three words.

The first revelation came from reading Genesis 3:15. When God cursed Satan for deceiving Adam and Eve, he said: "And I will put enmity between you and the woman, and between your offspring and hers; he will crush your head and you will strike his heel." Enmity is antagonism, hatred, fierce loathing. It became clear to me. There is enmity between Satan and women. The enemy of God hates women. He will do everything in his power to make women suffer, to make them ineffective, to debase them. Why? The reason is clear — it is through a woman that Jesus crushes [Satan's] head.

Through this I understood the call to "free the women" as a commandment to do spiritual battle: "For we wrestle not against flesh and blood but against principalities, against powers, against the rulers of the darkness of this world, against spiritual wickedness in high places" (Ephesians 6:12 KJV). Then came another revelation from the scriptures: Matthew 9:35-38:

> "Jesus went through all the towns and villages, teaching in their synagogues, proclaiming the good news of the kingdom and healing every disease and sickness. When He saw the crowds, He had compassion on them because they were harassed and helpless, like sheep without a shepherd. Then He said to His disciples, 'The harvest is plentiful, but the workers are few. Ask the Lord of the harvest, therefore, to send out workers into His harvest field.'"

Who is the Lord of the harvest? Our Good Shepherd — Jesus. Ask him what? To "send out workers into the harvest field." Why? Because "the harvest is plentiful," meaning many are seeking God. Who are the workers? His disciples. Who are these disciples? They are the men and women who accept Jesus as Lord and are willing to leave everything to follow him.

Jesus is not referring only to the Twelve Disciples here. He is referring to all his disciples; all those who follow him. This includes women. However, if women are not released or "freed" by the church to go into the harvest field or to follow the call of God for their lives, the workers will continue to be few. It is Satan's plan to keep women out of the harvest field. It is not God's plan.

According to the revealing article, *What Women Think of Faith, Leadership and Their Role in the Church* from Barna Research (2012)[2], women are "frustrated by their lack of opportunities at church and feel misunderstood and undervalued by their church leaders." Add to this the findings of the Pew Research Center's survey on religion outlined in its article, *America's Changing Religious Landscape* (2015), and the news is not good. "In the United States, Christians will decline from more than three-quarters of the population in 2010 to two-thirds in 2050…"[3]

The survey goes on to report that the number of the religiously unaffiliated (those who have no connection with religion) is growing throughout the country. The number of people saying they are unaffiliated is the highest since the survey began in 1934 (five percent in 1934 to 22.8 percent in 2014). This is nearly a quarter of the American population — a mission field equal to many foreign countries.

With such a need for the gospel in America, why is there such a lack of opportunity for women in the American church? Why would any church hamper the work of women who are called to be pastors, evangelists, or teachers when the harvest is so plentiful?

> "So Christ himself gave the apostles, the prophets, the evangelists, the pastors and teachers, to equip his people [men and women] for works of service, so that the body of Christ may be built up until we all reach unity in the faith and in the knowledge of the Son of God and become mature, attaining to the whole measure of the fullness of Christ.
>
> Then we will no longer be infants, tossed back and forth by the waves, and blown here and there by every wind of teaching and by the cunning and craftiness of people in their deceitful scheming. Instead, speaking the truth in love, we will grow to become in every respect the mature body of Him who is the head, that is, Christ." — Ephesians 4:11-15

The harvest is now plentiful and women need to be empowered by the church to become the apostles, the prophets, the evangelists, the pastors, the priests and the teachers, equipped by the church for works of service. They must not be treated like children by well-meaning church "parents" who impose strict rules on what women can be and do based on a few scriptures in the New Testament. These scriptures were not meant to curtail women's roles for all time but to support and instruct an infant church.

As a parent, my prime focus was to care for and protect my babies. I set strict barriers to keep them safe. As they grew, I removed the barriers and allowed them to walk freely through the house. When they got older, I opened the door and let them experience the outside world.

Throughout their development, I taught them, guided them and admonished them, providing them with tools for healthy, safe living. Then the day came when I handed them the keys to the car and allowed them free access to the world, knowing I had done my job as a parent, equipping them with everything they would need to become successful adults.

What kind of parent would I be if I kept my children as infants? Yes, they were cute and adorable at the baby stage, but once they grew up, treating them as infants would have been unnatural and against God's design. In fact, I would have created developmentally delayed, spiritually atrophied, bitter, dysfunctional adults of no use to the world — a travesty of wasted lives.

It is God's will, the design of Christ, to equip his church — its men and its women — with the tools to become healthy, strong, spirit-filled workers to reap the harvest. It is unnatural for the church to keep women as infants, refusing to allow them to move into leadership positions or to serve as apostles, prophets, evangelists, pastors, teachers, or priests — whatever be their calling.

It is time for the church to grow up as well. It is no longer an infant movement from the first century. It is more than 2,000 years old, certainly old enough to be considered mature. Now is the time for churches to "put aside childish things" and lift all prohibitions on women. No woman should be denied her spiritual calling because of her gender.

Please understand my intent. I am not suggesting every woman is called to positions of leadership, but those who are should not be hindered. Perhaps your calling is to raise children and be a helpmate to your husband or care for elderly parents or sick relatives. Your gifts may be creativity, generosity, intercession, or listening — gifts which should be viewed by the church as valued assets.

Jesus often met women in their domestic roles — mothering children, celebrating a wedding, fixing dinner for guests, or drawing water from a well. He was there for them in their time of need, when they were suffering from disease, oppressed by demons, desperate with a sick child, ostracized by society. He lifted them up in circumstances when they expected and received condemnation from the world — pregnant without marriage, caught in adultery, wasting expensive perfume. He saw their value, whether they were old or young.

As you read this book, may you find spiritual nourishment and encouragement in the certainty that God is personally interested in seeing you walk toward your destiny — to be all he created you to be. Thank God, for he has come so that we, all the redeemed, might be his voice to a fallen world, bringing his love, power, and glory. The harvest is plentiful. People are hungry for the Living God. It is time to send all laborers into the field.

Women of faith, it is time for you to answer the call of God. It is time to be accountable for your faith and seek your destiny. It is time to come face-to-face with Jesus and dedicate your life to serving him.

Sisters and brothers in Christ, I pray his Spirit will descend upon you and give you divine revelation as you explore these foundational encounters. May you discover that where the Spirit of the Lord is there is freedom.

~ ~ ~ ~ ~

You will seek me and find me when you seek me with all your heart.
— Jeremiah 29:13

I

MOTHER MARY: THE EARLY YEARS

Mary, the mother of Jesus, has been the subject of countless writings and sermons, but she remains a mystery to many of us. To some, she is a deity to worship and to others she is merely a womb for the Messiah. There has been so much written about Mary throughout the centuries; so many myths, extrapolations and worship, one hesitates to even address her role as a woman of the Gospels.

Whatever else she is, she is significant. Messiah, Emmanuel, Savior of mankind, Jesus of Nazareth was born of a woman and her name was Mary. She is the woman God chose in Genesis 3:15 to defeat Satan:

"And I will put enmity between you and the woman, and between your offspring and hers; he will crush your head and you will strike his heel."

For all her importance, she is mentioned only four times in the Gospels and once in the Epistles. According to Biblical scholars, she was a virgin between 12 and 14 years of age (the marriageable age at the time) living in the town of Nazareth in Galilee.

She was betrothed to a carpenter named Joseph when the angel

Gabriel materialized before her and told her she would give birth to the promised Messiah, who was to come from the line of David. It is generally believed that Mary's genealogy is given in Luke 3:23-38, while Joseph's is in Matthew 1:1-17. Whether from actual or legal lineage, Mary was descended from the House of David.[4]

MARY'S BABY AND CHILD

Mary enters our story with a visit from Gabriel, one of the great archangels, recorded in Luke 1:28-38:

> "The angel went to her and said, 'Greetings, you who are highly favored! The Lord is with you.' Mary was greatly troubled at his words and wondered what kind of greeting this might be. But the angel said to her, 'Do not be afraid, Mary; you have found favor with God. You will conceive and give birth to a son, and you are to call him Jesus. He will be great and will be called the Son of the Most High. The Lord God will give him the throne of his father David, and he will reign over Jacob's descendants forever; his kingdom will never end.'

> 'How will this be,' Mary asked the angel, 'since I am a virgin?' The angel answered, 'The Holy Spirit will come on you, and the power of the Most High will overshadow you. So the holy one to be born will be called the Son of God. Even Elizabeth your relative is going to have a child in her old age, and she who was said to be unable to conceive is in her sixth month. For no word from God will ever fail.

> "'I am the Lord's servant,' Mary answered. 'May your word to me be fulfilled.' Then the angel left her."

The passage most telling about Mary is when Gabriel declares she is "highly favored of God" as stated in Luke 1:29. Mary has an uncanny feeling about these words and is "troubled by them." Why? Would not being "highly favored" bring ecstatic praise? Why would she find these words troubling? It is not hard for us, as women, to understand that she found it difficult to believe she was "highly favored."

First, she was a woman living in a patriarchal culture and had no rights. Second, as far as we know, she had not done anything "religious" to prepare for God's favor. She had not performed the purification rituals or *mikvah* before this announcement (*mikvah* is the Jewish ritual of full immersion in water to make one's self pure before God). She had not done one significant deed to merit it. If God's favor were based on something she had done, the scriptures would have mentioned it. We would expect some telling example of what Mary had done to deserve being highly favored.

We know she came from a little town and most likely had no particular training or education. She was not a religious scholar. She was not wealthy. She was not a mature woman who had helped the poor and cared for the sick. All we know is she had done nothing special. Her most significant attribute is being a virgin — in other words, her greatest attribute is her lack of experience.

Third, based on Old Testament scriptures, only the patriarchs and mighty men of God such as Joseph, Moses and David were "highly favored." Being favored of God from Mary's perspective would have been troubling because she was not a religious leader, not well known, and not male. She is a young girl in a farming community, with only a modicum of religious training. She may have been devout, pure of heart and even physically attractive, but she has not done anything to warrant God's favor, which is the point. Mary, a woman, is the first to receive the unmerited favor of God under the New Covenant. Under the Old Covenant, she would not have been even counted among the populace.

Gabriel has yet to give her the big news, but Mary believed immediately that she was truly being visited by an angel and was humbled by his words. If the scriptures had not said she was "troubled" at these words, we might imagine she would act like any teenage girl who is told she is special. She would say, "I know. I am all that and then some!" However, she is not self-centered, she is humble. She must have been thinking, "Why me? Am I hearing him right? I'm nothing special." Her humility is endearing. Her spiritual sensitivity is impressive.

Because most scholars have deduced the marriageable age of females in Jesus' day was between the ages of 12 and 14, they accept it as fact that Mary is a pubescent girl when she receives this visitation from God's messenger. This might imply the One who created her is ignorant of all things female, which is a ridiculous assumption. As a woman, it is hard to believe a child barely experiencing the onset of her menses would be chosen for such a task — that God would choose a child to miraculously impregnate. This belief is offensive to women. What kind of God would disregard the tender mind and body of a child and put her at such risk, mentally, socially and physically?

As we will see in the story of Anna the prophet, when it is warranted, the Word will actually give the age. Anna was 84. In the story of Jairus' daughter, the scriptures are specific about her age: "She was twelve years old" (Mark 5:42). On this most singular event involving a woman in the Gospels, why is Mary's age left out? She represents the purity of all virgins who have not "known" a man; of all ages, through all time.

By reading the scriptures carefully, by listening to Mary's voice, we can ascertain from a female perspective that Mary was probably older than 12, even older than 13 or 14; most likely she was somewhere between 15 and 17. Puberty in girls begins as early as 10 but usually is completed by age 15 or 17.

If we remember when we were that age; even with the differences in culture, as females we are aware that we mature much faster than males do. Because of the radical changes to our bodies, thoughts of marriage and childbearing are entertained in our minds (whether to accept or reject). Our bodies force us to accept at an early age the rhythm of a monthly menstrual cycle; we develop breasts, painfully tender until we reach the end of puberty, we bleed but don't die, our bodies are mysterious and completely different from boys. Women understand the cycle of life at an early age.

When I was fifteen, I may not have been fully mature, but I was smart and self-aware. I had spiritual awareness; I had determined God existed. I knew if I had sexual relations, I could get pregnant. I knew what I wanted to be. I knew what I did not want to be. I had already planned my life.

The reason I am making such a point about Mary's age is that being female, I must believe the One who created me is not ignorant of what it is to be female. Gabriel tells Mary, "The Lord is with you." This indicates a relationship. The Lord knows Mary, and the Lord knows you — as a female. In the scriptures, we see Mary is someone who has her own mind, who is mature and devout, and who is knowledgeable enough of the prophecy regarding the Messiah to understand the significance of the angel's stunning words.

God loves Mary. He is intimately aware of Mary's state of mind, the state of her spirit and the readiness of her body. She is therefore not a pubescent girl, but a mature young woman who has put off marriage until ready to accept all of its responsibilities. God favors her. She has all the right ingredients: spiritually, emotionally, intellectually, and physically, to be selected as the one to bring the Messiah into the world.

Gabriel goes on to tell Mary that the Holy Spirit will come upon her and she will conceive through God's spirit not through the seed of a man. Shocking words, to be sure. She is betrothed, but she is a virgin. How is pregnancy going to be possible? You can imagine how her mind was reeling. She was a virgin, she would be made with child, and everyone would think she was unfaithful to her betrothed. Joseph would probably dissolve the betrothal and she would be an outcast, known as a whore. Under Mosaic Law, she could be stoned to death (Deuteronomy 22:23-24). But, what did Mary say? "I am the Lord's servant. May your word to me be fulfilled."

Mary makes all women marvel. She receives a visitation from one of the named angels of God — Gabriel probably appeared in human form, but surely was unlike any man she had seen before. As an unmarried female in a little town full of gossips, the presence of this "man" must have terrified her.

Yet Mary is serene. Her responses are not of fear or terror. The scripture does not say she ran, or cowered, or burst into tears. She responds with intelligence and confidence: "How will this be? I am a virgin." She is not afraid to dispute this heavenly being. She is not willing to accept his word. She is inquisitive. I like this about Mary. It must have taken some courage to respond this way. She is highly favored of God for a reason. She has a spiritual awareness; she is kind, pure and brave. God knew what establishing the New Covenant would cost his Son, and he knew what pain and suffering this young woman would endure as a result. God chose her for a reason.

The God of Heaven and Earth is on the move. The time has come for mankind's redemption. He has chosen a time and place to bring his Son into the physical world, and he has chosen a female to give Jesus life. Do you ever wonder why God chose to bring Jesus into the world in this way? He could have created Jesus fully grown and set him in the courts of Jerusalem to declare his Kingdom. The Jews certainly thought this was how it was going to be done. He could have created a baby to be found on a hillside by wandering shepherds. He could have come in the clouds in the full raiment of his glory. However, his plan was to bring forth the Messiah through the line of David. His plan, devised from the moment he created woman, was to have her "crush the head" of Satan.

Through this act, God validates and honors women and their importance, not as baby-making vehicles but as essential expressions of his creation. If Mary were only important because of a womb, he did not have to tell her. He could have told Joseph his betrothed was carrying the Messiah. If God thought about women as the men of that time did, he did not need to include Mary in his plans. He could have informed Joseph since Joseph came from the line of David. Nevertheless, he did tell Mary. God sent his greatest angel, Gabriel, to let Mary in on his plan.

As soon as the angel leaves her, Mary hurries to tell her cousin Elizabeth what has happened. She probably needs confirmation from a mature and strong female relative. When she sees her, Elizabeth immediately confirms it (Luke 1:43): "But why am I so favored, that the mother of my Lord should come to me?"

Mary is overjoyed and bursts into prophetic song.

This prophetic song reveals Mary's heart. She is devoted to God and has an understanding of his might and power. It is a song of true worship. It conveys her knowledge of the scripture revealing God's compassion for the poor, and Mary's own faith in the Messiah and what he will do. Her words give us an indication of what kind of person Mary is; she is not ignorant, childish, or frightened. She is full of the Spirit. When you read those words in Luke 1:46-55 you see a mature woman full of zeal and power:

> "And Mary said: 'My soul glorifies the Lord and my spirit rejoices in God my Savior, for he has been mindful of the humble state of his servant. From now on all generations will call me blessed, for the Mighty One has done great things for me — holy is his name.
>
> 'His mercy extends to those who fear him, from generation to generation. He has performed mighty deeds with his arm; he has scattered those who are proud in their inmost thoughts. He has brought down rulers from

their thrones but has lifted up the humble. He has filled
the hungry with good things but has sent the rich away
empty. He has helped his servant Israel, remembering to
be merciful to Abraham and his descendants forever, just
as he promised our ancestors.'"

Three months later, Mary returns home to face her family and Joseph,
her betrothed. This would have required tremendous courage, but her
faith had been made strong by her time with Elizabeth.

In Matthew's Gospel (1:19), we know Mary faced censure because
once Joseph realized she was pregnant he planned to divorce her quietly.
An angel appears to him in a dream and changes his mind, saying "Joseph
son of David, do not be afraid to take Mary home as your wife, because
what is conceived in her is from the Holy Spirit" (v. 20). The scriptures
go on to say Joseph obeys and has no relations with Mary until after
Jesus is born.

When Mary is in the advanced stage of her pregnancy, what should
happen but Caesar Augustus' decision to have a census, requiring every
person to travel to his or her hometown to be counted. Keep in mind
this is the same Mary who spoke with an angel and prophesied about
the might of God. She is a practical, intelligent and courageous young
woman of faith, but even so, she must have wondered if she would have
to give birth on the side of the road.

Can you imagine being in your ninth month of pregnancy and having to
ride on a donkey for eighty miles? Moreover, once she arrives in Bethlehem
she and Joseph find there is no decent lodging available and they must
stay in a stable with smelly, dirty farm animals. We know Mary was a
woman of faith and courage, but her heart must have broken to think of
giving birth to the Messiah on a bed of straw. Did she have doubts at this
time? Did she wonder if God was actually with her? It may have been a
frustrating, depressing, disheartening moment in her life.

Even so, Mary was close to God and had a spirit of resiliency. She proved to have an indomitable spirit making the best of every situation. She could have said to Joseph, "How perfect. Now when I go into labor I won't wake the other guests" or "think how much money we've saved this way."

We don't have a clue what Mary really thought, but as women we can sympathize with her situation and imagine ourselves faced with difficulties and challenges which, on the surface, make apparent that God has abandoned us. Mary endured incredible hardships. Being favored of God did not mean she would not suffer. In fact, she would endure greater sufferings than these.

After Jesus is born, shepherds and Magi come to see what God has declared through heavenly hosts and prophecy. Whether Mary is aware of it or not, supernatural things are happening all around her — a bright star appears in the sky, choirs of angels, strangers bearing gifts for a king — and the Word says, "…and Mary treasured up all these things and pondered them in her heart" (Luke 2:19).

I have always loved this scripture. It is as if Mary is unfazed by all the fuss, but accepts and imprints the signs on her heart. Holding her newborn son must have felt like the greatest miracle of all time. Knowing as she did he is to be the Messiah would have made the experience unutterably precious. A healthy child, a safe birth, a faithful mate; these are miracles which happen every second in the world today. Let us treasure and ponder all of these in our own hearts.

Why was this scripture included in the narrative of Jesus' birth? It is included because Mary would go with her son to the cross and beyond, and it gives us a clue to her thinking. This is an aspect of womanhood important for us to recognize. Women remember. Women keep track of the important events in their lives. They remember birthdays, anniversaries, the first word, the first step, the first tooth. They treasure these moments so in times of trouble they can remember the small miracles and find strength to endure.

As the mother of Jesus, Mary did not have it easy. Her son is an extraordinary child. When Jesus is taken to Jerusalem for purification, a devout man, Simeon, takes Mary aside and prophesies to her, saying, "this child is destined to cause the falling and rising of many in Israel, and to be a sign that will be spoken against, so that the thoughts of many hearts will be revealed. And a sword will pierce your own soul too" (Luke 2:34-35). This is a message for Mary's ears alone; to prepare her for what is to come. It must have caused her great concern.

As a mother, you will do anything to protect your child, but this child, this Jesus, was unlike any other. His life would not be smooth. He would be controversial, and there is an indication he will die young, an occurrence that will "pierce her soul." Mary will remember these words, and she will see them come to pass. She will also remember the words of the angel Gabriel, "For no word from God will ever fail" (Luke 1:37).

Later on, during another journey to Jerusalem for the Passover, the young Jesus slips out from under his parents' control and disappears into the temple court (Luke 2:41-52). He would have been about twelve years old and by this time, Mary would have had other children to care for. We know from scripture that she had four more sons and at least two daughters as is indicated in Matthew 13:55-56a: "Is not this the carpenter's son? Is not his mother called Mary and his brethren, James, and Joses, and Simon and Judas? And his sisters, are they not all with us?"

On such a long journey with so many people traveling together, it is easy to see how she could have lost track of Jesus. I would surmise her firstborn was often disappearing and was rather independent. She had her hands full, and may even have been pregnant at the time when Jesus disappeared in Jerusalem for five days. She must have been beside herself with worry.

I remember when my own sons went missing for five hours. They were six and seven years old and were playing in the backyard as I was preparing dinner. When dinner was ready, I called them in, but they were no longer in the backyard. I walked up and down the streets calling their names, but they did not come. With every passing minute, my mind filled with horrifying images. I even imagined their funerals and how devastated I would be. We called the police and alerted them that two young boys were missing. Officers came out immediately and questioned us.

As I paced and cried, the police combed the area. It was now dark and I was frantic. Three hours later, the police arrived with the boys in tow. They had been playing in the backyard of one of their friends and didn't notice night had fallen. My sons were oblivious to the panic they had caused me. But I never forgot how my mind spun during those hours.

I'm sure Mary felt the same when she realized her precious firstborn was missing after a whole day of travel, then a whole day back to Jerusalem and three more days of scouring the streets before finding him calmly sitting in the temple courts, confounding the teachers with his questions and answers. He was completely oblivious to his parents' worry.

With childlike surprise, Jesus responded to their chastisement, "Why? Didn't you know I'd be in my Father's house?" The scriptures state Mary and Joseph did not know what he was talking about, but I have a suspicion Mary felt the first stab of foreknowledge pierce her heart. All the way back to Nazareth, she must have felt a mixture of pride and worry as she thought about what had happened. If I were Mary, from then on I would have kept a sharp eye on this child. She knew he was different, but she may not have realized how different until that moment in the temple.

The scriptures (Luke 2:51-52) state when Jesus rejoined his parents, he was "obedient to them" from then on and "grew in wisdom and stature and in favor with God and men." In other words, Jesus was smart, healthy, and people liked him. He had the discernible favor of God. He was also Mary's son and realized how terrified she had been when he disappeared for five days. He loved his mother. Throughout the scriptures, we see evidence of Jesus' love for his mother, particularly at the end.

However, let us not forget Mary was a real woman in a real time.

Into his adulthood, Jesus lived with Mary. They had a mother and son relationship. She was constantly aware Jesus was the Son of the Most High God because she had experienced a supernatural pregnancy. She would have remembered the promise she had received from the angel Gabriel that "The Lord God will give him the throne of his father David, and he will reign over Jacob's descendants forever" (Luke 1:32-33).

Yet, according to the scriptures, we know Jesus is still living at home well into his late twenties. She must have wondered then when his reign was to start. All of his friends would have taken up their lives; married, had children, engaged in meaningful work. As far as we know, Jesus has done none of these normal Jewish male things. Do you think Mary pushed him out of the nest as any good Jewish mother would do? Is it possible she said to him, "Now, Jesus, it's time for you to start reigning. You can always come home for a visit, but it's time to spread your wings."

THE WEDDING IN CANA

The next time we hear about Mary she is at a wedding in Cana. We get a different impression of her from John 2:1-12:

> "On the third day a wedding took place at Cana in Galilee. Jesus's mother was there, and Jesus and his disciples had also been invited to the wedding. When the wine was gone, Jesus's mother said to Him, 'They have no more wine.'
>
> 'Woman, why do you involve me?' Jesus replied. 'My hour has not yet come.'
>
> "His mother said to the servants, 'Do whatever He tells you.'
>
> Nearby stood six stone water jars, the kind used by the

Jews for ceremonial washing, each holding from twenty to thirty gallons. Jesus said to the servants, 'Fill the jars with water;' so they filled them to the brim. Then He told them, 'now draw some out and take it to the master of the banquet.'

They did so, and the master of the banquet tasted the water turned into wine. He did not realize where it had come from, though the servants who had drawn the water knew. Then he called the bridegroom aside and said, 'Everyone brings out the choice wine first and then the cheaper wine after the guests have had too much to drink; but you have saved the best till now.'

What Jesus did here in Cana of Galilee was the first of the signs through which He revealed His glory; and His disciples believed in Him. After this he went down to Capernaum with His mother and brothers and His disciples. There they stayed for a few days."

Mary has grown up. From all we can gather from these scriptures, Mary and Jesus are guests at the Cana wedding. We know his ministry has begun because his disciples are there. This would mean Mary is now in her early forties and will have a number of grown children. She may even be a grandmother by this time. She has taken her rightful place as the matriarch of the family. She expects to be obeyed, or at least respected and honored. There is authority in her words and by her son's reaction, we get a glimpse of their relationship.

In John 2:3, Mary speaks to Jesus and says, "They have no more wine." What is implied in these words? It is such a matter-of-fact statement we can only gather she expects Jesus to do something about the situation. Jesus has not yet operated in the miraculous. He is a phenomenal speaker, persuasive and charismatic. He has a number of followers. He is making news, so to speak. Yet he is only seen as an up-and-coming rabbi with a singular ability to interpret scripture and illuminate the law. However, Mary knows something about him no one else does.

Mary never forgets, but "treasures all these things" about Jesus in her heart. We do not have any examples of Jesus performing miracles as a child or as a young man. Nevertheless, from Mary's point of view, she knows He is capable of it. When the wine gives out, she goes to him and suggests he create a miracle. "They have no more wine." And Jesus appears shocked by her suggestion. He has not created any miracles publicly before, and now his mother asks him to make wine.

He responds, "Why do you involve me? My hour has not yet come" (v. 4). However, she does involve him. Perhaps she has been waiting all these years for her son to fulfill the promise God gave her. She knows he is a "supernatural" child. His conception, his birth, his unique personality, his phenomenal dissertations in the Temple as a child, and all the prophesies from family and strangers have affirmed that he is the Messiah; these are things she has treasured in her heart and she believes without a doubt her son is the Son of God. If the Son of God cannot do something about the wine, then he is not supernaturally inclined.

I do not believe Mary doubted Jesus' ability to remedy the wine situation. Her statement is so cut and dried. "Son, they're out of wine. Fix things." Is it possible she was only asking him to go out and borrow or buy some wine? Take a collection from all his friends and disciples and refill the supply? No. Mary is pressing Jesus to act supernaturally.

We can discern this because of Jesus' reaction. He immediately understands she is not asking him to replenish the wine supply by natural means. He knows she is asking him for a miracle. As any good mother will do, Mary is pressuring her son to stretch himself toward his destiny. In Mary's view, this is a simple opportunity for Jesus to prove who he is.

However, by Jesus' reaction, we get the sense he does not see it that way. He says, "My hour has not yet come." What does he mean? He knows what the end of his life will be and has no desire to hasten it. He appears reluctant to take the next step. Mary is his mother. She knows him better than anyone else does. He sees the end result; she sees the beginning. It is as if she is saying to him, "Now is the time." She does not accept his inclination to delay.

In verse 5, she turns to the servants and says, "Do whatever he tells you." She has now put him on the spot. You can imagine the servants are all looking at Jesus with expectation. What can he do? It will dishonor his mother if he says, "not now." Mary has put him in a situation in which he must obey her or shame her. He is a good son. He is an obedient son. He loves and honors his mother.

Immediately, in verse 7, Jesus turns to the servants and says, "Fill the jars with water." He obeys his mother. Whether he does it reluctantly or with a smile on his face, we know he performs a miracle. The jars are filled with water and he commands them to be drawn out and taken to the master of the banquet. He doesn't test it first. He doesn't ask his mother to see if it "worked." He is fully capable of doing the miraculous. Mary knows it. He knows it. He sends the servants to the master of the banquet. He does not expect him to say, "Why have you brought me water?" He performs a simple but incredible, miraculous act at the prompting of his mother. Mary, a mere woman, propels Jesus into the supernatural through her faith.

~ ~ ~ ~ ~

MEDITATION

Mary raised her blessed child from birth to adulthood. It couldn't have been easy for her. She loved Jesus and yet he "pierced her heart" on more than one occasion. Think of your own mother. Have your actions ever wounded her — intentionally or unintentionally? Seek the Lord for wisdom on how to honor your mother and, if you are a mother, how to raise your children to serve the Lord.

> *"If any of you lacks wisdom, you should ask God, who gives generously to all without finding fault, and it will be given to you." — James 1:5*

> *"Truly I am your servant, Lord; I serve you just as my mother did; you have freed me from my chains." — Psalms 116:16*

Study Guide Questions

MOTHER MARY: THE EARLY YEARS

— List three things you want to remember about Mary, the mother of Jesus.

— In the Christian faith, there is no woman more venerated worldwide than the Virgin Mary. Discuss her importance while respecting the views of others.

— What kind of relationship does Mary have with God? How does knowing this help you with your own relationship with God?

— Jesus performed his first public miracle at the wedding of Cana. What role did his mother Mary play in this? Is it important? Why?

— What do you think Mary "treasured in her heart" regarding her son? How do you think these treasured experiences prepared her for the future?

— Mary accepted God's plan for her life, knowing she could be misunderstood, excluded or even killed. Discuss how knowing this helps you in your life and/or your ministry?

NOTES

II

MOTHER MARY: THE SILENT YEARS

As a child, Jesus grew in favor with God and man and his mother Mary was by his side, guiding and teaching him, preparing him for his destiny. She grew older, more mature and wise. From the moment Jesus performs his public miracle at the wedding in Cana, his ministry becomes explosive. He is in high demand and great crowds follow him everywhere.

In the Bible, Mary is silent throughout Jesus' ministry. We do not hear her voice again. She plays no other role than silent observer to the unfolding events she has known about since his birth. However, Mary is not silent because she is seen as insignificant.

Remember her prophetic song: "from now on all generations will call me blessed, for the Mighty One has done great things for me" (Luke 1:48-49). Mary's part in the birth and upbringing of Jesus has been remembered and honored for thousands of years.

We know from her interaction with him at the wedding in Cana she is aware of his supernatural abilities. She has launched her son as best she can and now her role as guide has ended. We do not know how Mary felt about this. The scriptures nearly drop her from any further mention. More than likely, she returns to her home in Nazareth and takes up her duties as a devout Jewish mother.

If you are a mother of grown children, perhaps you understand why Mary loses her voice at this time. The role of mothers is to nurture, train and launch their children into productive adult lives. Good mothers will let go and trust in their training when their children have reached adulthood. Mary is a good mother. She gives Jesus the final push in Cana and then goes home to take care of her other children and grandchildren and to keep the family going. Her influence on her son resides no longer in her ability to instruct him but in his love for her.

I remember the moment when I realized my ability to instruct my youngest son was gone. After years of telling him what to do and guiding his thoughts and actions, it was hard for me to accept my motherly advice was no longer welcome. It was not that my son did not love or respect me, but in order to assert his own individuality, he needed to disconnect from his dependence on me. He wanted — he needed — to make his own decisions.

I did not like what he was doing with his life. I had other ideas for him. As far as I was concerned, his life as a professional skydiver was dangerous and superficial. We would get into intense arguments due to my desire to change his mind. The more I pressed, the more resistant he became.

I will never forget the moment when he said to me on the phone after another battle of wills: "Mom, you told me to pursue my dreams and love what I do. This is what I'm doing, and if you can't accept this, you and I will drift further and further apart." The thought of us drifting apart was more terrifying than my fear about what he was doing. I booked the next flight to California and lived with him on the drop zone for two weeks to experience the world that had captured his heart.

It was a great learning experience for me. I came to see my work as his mother as complete. I learned to accept my son in the entirety of his life. I learned to step back as a mother and become his friend and confidant. It changed how we related to each other. From then on, our deep love for one another was expanded by a deeper respect. My influence over him was negligible, but when it came to his love for me, I had an overabundance.

Even though my fear was eventually realized, I cannot dismiss the love we shared or the joy he felt doing what he was doing. In 2009, my beloved son died parachuting over the Eiger in Switzerland for a movie. When news of his death came to me, I was devastated even though I "knew" when he left he would not return. I cannot explain it except as a foreboding that wouldn't go away. I couldn't change the outcome. I can deeply relate to Mary and how she knew very early on that her son was going to die young.

The scriptures do not say Mary is a widow, but we can speculate that she is. After the incident in the synagogue when Jesus was twelve, we don't learn anything more about Joseph. All we know is he was a devout man, followed the law, worked as a carpenter, and may have had children with Mary (or he had children from a previous marriage — Joseph may have been much older and a widower with grown children). We presume he died sometime before Jesus' ministry begins because his sons, Jesus' brothers, are named and mentioned as being with Mary but not with Joseph. It is most likely Joseph has died and they are now taking care of Mary, possibly working as carpenters themselves.

As firstborn, Jesus' responsibility would have been to care for his widowed mother. His siblings may have had some resentment toward him as a result. Regardless, Mary's other children (or her stepchildren) take care of her, while her "supernatural" child is traveling the country, becoming famous and dangerously controversial. The next reference to Mary is in Mark 3:31-35 (this account is also recorded in Matthew 12:46-50), in which it is stated:

"Then Jesus' mother and brothers arrived. Standing outside, they sent someone in to call Him. A crowd was sitting around Him, and they told Him, 'Your mother and brothers are outside looking for you.'

'Who are my mother and my brothers?' He asked. Then He looked at those seated in a circle around Him and said, 'Here are my mother and my brothers! Whoever does God's will is my brother and sister and mother.'"

In these passages, Jesus does not refer to his earthly "father," which indicates Joseph may no longer be living. He does, however, mention "sister," indicating he has sisters, and they are outside with his mother and brothers. He may also be referring to the women who are seated near him in the house.

It is enjoyable for me to know Jesus had sisters. In Matthew 13:56, the people from his hometown mention these sisters as proof he is only an ordinary man: "Aren't all His sisters with us?" We do not know if these "sisters" are older or younger. If they came from Joseph's first marriage, they could be older. If they are Mary and Joseph's children, they would be younger. At least we know from the scriptures that Jesus had more than one sister. This is a further indication that in his dealings with people, Jesus is all-inclusive. If in Mark 3:35 he is actually referring to the women seated around him, then Jesus is including females as well as males in his kingdom if they "do God's will."

It is surprising that Jesus takes this stance toward his mother and siblings. After all, they only want to speak to him. Why must he seem to publicly disown them? He is an obedient son, so why is he showing disrespect to his mother. Or is he? What is really going on here?

We must look at this passage in the context of where Jesus is in his ministry. He is in his full adult spiritual power, performing miracles. Wherever he goes, he heals all who are sick. Incredible acts are being reported: the lame walk, the blind see, the mute speak, lepers are made clean. No matter where Mary and her children are, word of Jesus' works must have reached them through the testimonies and simple gossip of others

Mary also must have heard Elizabeth's son, John, is in prison. Everyone thinks John is safe and untouchable. He is a holy man. He has a large following. Nevertheless, John has made an enemy of King Herod and has suffered the consequences. Mary does not want to see her own son suffer the same way. She probably recalls Simeon's ominous prophecy (Luke 2:34-35).

Before her next encounter with her son, the rumor is that Jesus has called out the Pharisees for their hypocrisy. It is not surprising that Mary realizes Jesus has made powerful enemies who will want to kill him. They have even declared Jesus is operating under Satan's power.

These rumors must have filled Mary with dread. Even though she has the assurance of her own experiences — Jesus is the promised Messiah — she is not a woman to sit by and let something terrible happen to her son. She may have considered the thought he will die before his time, but she clings to the belief he will yet rise in power and live to reign. Even Mary could not have known God's plan for Jesus to die on the cross for the atonement of all. Mary expects Jesus to reign in an earthly sense. Whether she is persuaded by her family or feels the need, she travels from Nazareth to speak with him.

Because they arrive at the house where Jesus is teaching, we can surmise Jesus' brothers are the ones who have brought the news to Mary. They may have even tried to persuade Jesus to lay low for awhile, and, as a last ditch effort, sought out their mother who has more influence on their brother. On the other hand, they might have ulterior motives. Maybe they feel he is embarrassing the family. Maybe they are jealous of all the attention he is getting when he should be home taking care of their mother. Whatever their motives, their purpose is to dissuade Jesus from his ministry and they bring their mother with them to accomplish that goal.

In Mark 3:21, there is a more concrete interpretation: "When His family heard about this, they went to take charge of Him, for they said, 'He is out of His mind.'" According to Mark's Gospel, even Jesus' family thinks he is crazy. I cannot believe this of Mary. She has prior knowledge of Jesus' special destiny and has seen with her own eyes and heard with her own ears how different and special her firstborn son is and has "treasured all these things in her heart." Therefore, we can speculate it is actually his brothers, and possibly even his sisters, who think he is crazy and they feel compelled to use their mother to influence him. They know Jesus loves her and believe she may be able to persuade him to alter his actions.

Imagine their surprise when Jesus refuses to come outside and, in fact, tells perfect strangers he does not acknowledge his siblings and mother as his family. Jesus knows their intent and he is not about to stop his ministry because of what they think about him. There is no mention in the scriptures that he came out to speak with his family. On the contrary, he stays where he is and speaks to the crowd around him. He does not want to rebuke his family publicly, and he does not want to confront his mother. Out of respect for her, he stays within the house and does not see them.

Nevertheless, his words are clear. His "family" is not an earthly family. His family are those who "do God's will." Leaving his followers and going home with his siblings and mother would not be God's will and he knows it. He must have been grieved to realize his own earthly family has come to dissuade him from his ministry. Their lack of faith probably made him sad.

Soon afterward, he leaves the house and goes to sit by a lake. A large crowd follows him. His tone and manner have now changed. Following the brusque statements made in the house when approached by his family, he seems to become contemplative and poetic. He conveys great spiritual mysteries veiled in a number of parables: the parable of the sower, the parable of the weeds, the parable of the mustard seed, the parable of hidden treasure and the pearl, the parable of the lamp, and the parable of the net. All these parables pertain to those who hear the Word, accept it, and live by faith and those who do not. Is his earthly family, those who came to "take charge of Him," on his mind when he reveals these parables?

Right at the beginning of the parables, he quotes from the prediction of the prophet Isaiah in fulfillment of prophecy, "You will be ever hearing but never understanding; you will be ever seeing but never perceiving. For this people's heart has become calloused; they hardly hear with their ears, and they have closed their eyes. Otherwise, they might see with their eyes, hear with their ears, understand with their hearts and turn, and I would heal them" (Isaiah 6:9-10 and Matthew 13:14-15).

Is he thinking of his own mother, brothers and sisters? I think he is fully aware of them when he relates these amazing parables. He is aware of his "separateness" even as he speaks. He is no longer simply a carpenter's son, a brother, a Nazarene. He is the Son of God. Filled with the Holy Spirit, he imparts powerful stories to wrestle with regarding the Kingdom of God.

The time frames differ between Matthew's and Mark's accounts, but sometime after this Jesus returns to his hometown. It is interesting that he does not speak to his family when they have traveled to see him but goes right afterward to Nazareth where they live. However, as far as we know, he does not go to his house. He is drawn to his hometown, but he does not feel connected any longer with his family. Instead, he goes to the synagogue and teaches there.

His mother, brothers, and sisters must have heard Jesus is in town. Did they come out to hear him speak? Were they angry, scared, disgusted, or confused? Why didn't he visit them first? There is no reference to his brothers coming to hear him speak. But maybe they did. Maybe their public humiliation was enough to make them examine their hearts. Maybe as they walked home with their mother, she told them what God had revealed to her about Jesus.

Whether from Mary's words or Jesus' ministry, we know through the Apostle Paul's writings that at least one of Jesus' brothers, James, became a follower (Galatians 1:18-19), and in Acts 1:14, it appears more of his brothers became believers. However, initially this was not the case.

In Matthew 13:54-58 (also Mark 6:1-6), the scriptures state:

> "Coming to His hometown, He began teaching the people in their synagogue, and they were amazed. 'Where did this man get this wisdom and these miraculous powers?' they asked. 'Isn't this the carpenter's son? Isn't His mother's name Mary, and aren't His brothers James, Joseph, Simon and Judas? Aren't all His sisters with us? Where then did this man get all these things?'

> "And they took offense at Him. But Jesus said to them, 'A prophet is not without honor except in his own town and in his own home.' And He did not do many miracles there, because of their lack of faith."

Jesus has returned home, but he is not honored and his work seems an offense to his family and neighbors. The reality of his parables is played out in Nazareth. He performs few miracles because of their unbelief. It says in Mark 6:6 "He is amazed at their lack of faith." He never returns.

AT THE CROSS

In John 19:25-27, we read that Mary stands at the foot of the cross in the company of other women and the Apostle John.

> "Near the cross of Jesus stood his mother, his mother's sister, Mary the wife of Clopas, and Mary Magdalene. When Jesus saw His mother there, and the disciple whom he loved standing nearby, he said to her, 'Woman, here is

your son,' and to John, 'Here is your mother.' From that time on, the disciple John took her into his home."

From the time Mary tries to speak to him at the insistence of her family to this terrible moment when she sees him hanging on the cross, there is no reference to Mary. Where is she all this time? We do not know. We do not know if she follows Him like the other women or stays in Nazareth until his crucifixion, but through this scripture, we know she is there at the beginning and she is there at the end.

How is it we find her at the foot of the cross in his final moments? I think as his mother she has been aware of him throughout his ministry, even if she is not walking in his footsteps. Someone must have told her he has been arrested. The news would come swiftly to her ears. As any mother, she goes to be with her son. Imagine what it is like for her to be waiting outside, not knowing what is happening to him, and then seeing him bloodied beyond recognition, paraded through the streets carrying the crossbeam for the crucifixion. Simeon's prophecy is fulfilled: Her heart is pierced.

We know at some point she makes her way to Golgotha and stands with Clopas' wife, Mary Magdalene, and John as a witness to her son's execution. There is no mention of the other apostles or Mary's other children being present. Granted, at this moment, all eyes are fixed on Jesus and no one is taking attendance. It is only because John records Jesus' final words that we learn his mother is there.

In great agony, Jesus speaks to Mary. Where before he had asked, "Who is my mother?" he now makes clear his mother is on his mind during his final moments. As her firstborn son, Jesus takes time to arrange for her care. He entrusts her to John, not to his own brothers and sisters. Everyone has scattered, not wanting to be further associated with him, but John and these women stand with him in solidarity.

When he addresses them, Jesus does not say, "Mother, here is your son." He says, "Woman, here is your son." Is he denying she is his mother?

I do not believe so. Most followers believe he is telling Mary that John is now to be her son and John will look after her. But, because he calls her "woman," we could also interpret his statement differently.

Could it be he is now calling her "woman" rather than mother because she has come to represent the universal woman? Could we, as women, not look at these words and interpret them as, "Women, here I am, the Son of God, and I die for you as well." Women are sanctified by Christ's sacrifice, as are men. To John, Jesus says, "Here is your mother," giving him the charge to accept, respect and honor the female. We again learn through Mary that God uses women in his divine plans.

John does not record any words spoken by Mary. The only sounds she may be making are gut-wrenching cries of horror and grief. It is impossible to imagine what she is thinking when she sees this terrible end to her son; how all the mystical experiences, prophesies, and miracles associated with him have come to this.

She surely recalls Gabriel's words to her at the beginning: "He will be great and will be called the Son of the Most High. The Lord God will give Him the throne of His father David, and He will reign over Jacob's descendants forever; His kingdom will never end" (Luke 1:31-33). How can these words compare to the sight before Mary's eyes?

Does she think of what Simeon said when Jesus was but two months old: "For my eyes have seen your salvation, which you have prepared in the sight of all nations: a light for revelation to the Gentiles, and the glory of your people Israel" (Luke 2: 30-32), how he stood in the temple of Jerusalem and confounded the rabbis, how miracle upon miracle had been attributed to him over the past three years. And when they thrust the sword into his side, did she remember Simeon saying, "and a sword will pierce your soul, too."

Mary was chosen to bring the Messiah into the world. Faced with the impossibility of conception without a male partner, she accepted God could make the impossible possible. Mary was a woman of faith.

Her natural eyes showed her a gruesome sight, but her spirit must have exerted tremendous faith that God could change this situation. Had she heard what he said; that he would be raised again in three days?

I believe God filled her with the grace of his Holy Spirit to help her endure and to keep faith even while she looked upon the horrible death of her son.Since John's Gospel states that from then on John takes care of Mary, it is not hard to imagine she was one of the first to know that Jesus was alive after John entered the empty tomb. Do you think he would not have told her?

Can you imagine Mary's feelings when she heard the news? Would she have raised her voice in prophetic song as she did earlier in her youth? Perhaps when they told her she said, "I have known it all along. Listen to what God told me from the beginning." Simply because her words are not recorded does not mean Mary is silent when she hears the news. I cannot imagine any mother being quiet at such a moment.

We know she continues as an active follower because in Acts 1:12-14 we learn Mary is with the apostles in the upper room at Pentecost: "Then the apostles returned to Jerusalem… [and] went upstairs to the room where they were staying... they all joined together constantly in prayer, along with the women and Mary the mother of Jesus, and with His brothers."

This is the last reference to Mary in the Bible. As the mother of Jesus, everyone who met her revered her. She must have told her story over and over, which was orally transmitted until Matthew, Mark, Luke, and John wrote it down. Women for centuries have relived Mary's experience and are able to draw strength, courage, and joy from her. She was "highly favored of God" and extends blessings to us even today.

~ ~ ~ ~ ~

MEDITATION

Throughout her life, Mary received grace and strength to face daunting events through the power of the Holy Spirit. If you are facing frustrations, difficulties, or grief, meditate on Mary's life and ask for the covering of the Holy Spirit and God's favor. You are a daughter of God and also highly favored.

May the Lord direct your hearts into God's love and Christ's perseverance. — 2 Thessalonians 3:5

Study Guide Questions

MOTHER MARY: THE SILENT YEARS

— List three things you want to remember about the silent Mother Mary.

— Mary accepted God's plan for her life, knowing she could be misunderstood, excluded or even killed. Discuss how knowing this helps you in your life and/or your ministry?

— Mary was wise enough to know when she had finished her work as a mother. Discuss the wisdom of knowing when to "let go" either from your own mother or from your own children. How will this help your spiritual walk?

— Losing a child is devastating. Discuss how you, your group, or your church can provide solace to a grieving mother. Devise two plans that can be implemented.

— Mary and other women were present in the "upper room" at Pentecost. How does this inclusion change the way you think about evangelism or church leadership?

— How does your church provide support to mothers? Is there more to be done? Come up with some practical ways to elevate the status of mothers.

NOTES

III

ELIZABETH

Elizabeth's distinctive role in the gospel story is inspiring and serves as an important transition from the Old Testament to the New Testament. She is the mother of John the Baptist and a cousin of Jesus' mother, Mary. Her relationship with her husband and parallel pregnancy with Mary give us insight into the heart of God for women.

When Mary visits Elizabeth, we see a strong connection between these women. Not only are they genetically related, but Mary also tells Elizabeth what has happened to her before telling anyone else. It is as if she cannot wait. Out of all her female relatives — her mother, sisters, aunts, or grandmothers — she wants first to tell her eldest cousin, Elizabeth, who lives "in the hill country of Judea" some distance away. She knows her cousin will understand and will believe her. We can surmise Mary is aware that Elizabeth is an especially spiritual woman, married to a priest, who practices mercy and love.

The scriptures state Elizabeth is a descendant of Aaron, the first high priest. She comes from a priestly line. Even though she does not perform priestly duties like Miriam, the sister of Aaron, Elizabeth has a priest's heart for God. Childless, she devotes her life to serving and worshipping God. In Luke 1:5-7, we learn exactly who Elizabeth is:

> "In the time of Herod king of Judea there was a priest named Zechariah, who belonged to the priestly division of Abijah; his wife, Elizabeth, was also a descendant of Aaron. Both of them were righteous in the sight of God, observing all the Lord's commands and decrees blamelessly. But they were childless because Elizabeth was not able to conceive, and they were both very old."

We do not know how old "very old" is, but more than likely Elizabeth is past her childbearing years, possibly over forty. Because she does not accompany Jesus at any point in his ministry, it is possible that she is either too old to travel or dead by that time. We do not know any more about Elizabeth than what is in this story, except that her son John becomes an adult and fulfills his calling as the herald of the Messiah. He will bring thousands of Jews to repentance and baptize them, preparing them for Jesus' arrival.

Unlike Mary's visitation, the archangel Gabriel appears to Elizabeth's husband Zechariah while he is performing priestly works in the temple, burning incense in the Holy of Holies. Gabriel informs him that Elizabeth will conceive and the boy's name will be John. He goes on to give Zechariah specific instructions about John and ends with an amazing declaration: "He will go on before the Lord, in the spirit and power of Elijah, to turn the hearts of the parents to their children and the disobedient to the wisdom of the righteous — to make ready a people prepared for the Lord" (Luke 1:17).

Zechariah (which means "God remembers") questions Gabriel as Mary did. "How can this be? My wife and I are old." However, Gabriel does something completely different with Zechariah. Mary is given voice while Zechariah's voice is suddenly silenced. God can do anything he wants. He can give voice to women and silence men, depending on the state of their hearts. To God, gender does not matter; the heart does.

Whereas Mary's question came from her faith, Zechariah's originated from skepticism or from a bruised male ego. He cannot believe what he is hearing. Elizabeth is barren. It is a source of great shame in his life. A man's ability to produce children represents his manhood — the more children, the greater the man. To produce no children at all is a sign of weakness, disfavor, or shame. It matters not that Zechariah is caught off guard by the "presence" in the Holy of Holies — forbidden to all except the designated priest, and, in this case, Zechariah — but Gabriel immediately hits the sorest spot in the man's soul: "Do not be afraid, Zechariah; your prayer has been heard. Your wife Elizabeth will bear you a son, and you are to call him John" (Luke 1:13).

The angel does not say, "Do not be afraid, Zechariah, you will have a son" or "you and Elizabeth are going to have a son." He says, "Your wife Elizabeth will bear you a son." Given what transpires, we surmise Zechariah did not respond in a positive way to this news. What is this angel suggesting? That he does not have what it takes to produce an heir, but maybe someone else can?

Gabriel also informs Zechariah that he isn't even going to be able to name his own child. He has been waiting a long time for an heir. He has tried on many names, and the greatest blessing in the world will be to name his son. But God tells him what to name the boy. "You will call him John." Not a lofty, priestly name, but a short, chopped-up name, one of the most common at that time, and one which doesn't even exist in his family line. (The name John means "the Lord has shown favor".)

We know this is important because later in the scriptures there is some question of what the baby's name will be and when Zechariah finally confirms his boy's name as John, his tongue is instantly loosed and he is able to speak. We do not know what Zechariah was thinking at the time Gabriel confronted him. We do know that even though his response is similar to Mary's, the result is completely different. That is because God knows what is in the heart.

Zechariah returns home completely mute, sorely humbled by his encounter with Gabriel and overwhelmed by the angel's prophecy. His lips are struck silent but his mind is reeling. He is unable to tell his wife what has happened. Their relationship must have changed after he returned home. Being mute prevented Zechariah from talking, which I think he was fond of doing, and he has to express himself in another way. They have relations and, miracle of miracles, old, barren Elizabeth conceives, not by the Holy Spirit as with Mary, but by divine intervention. In the midst of Zechariah's confusion and humility, there is great joy. Elizabeth is pregnant. This miracle must have shocked and amazed all those who knew the barren couple. It is obvious that God has intervened.

In Luke 1:24-25, we read: "After this his wife Elizabeth became pregnant and for five months remained in seclusion. 'The Lord has done this for me,' she said. 'In these days He has shown his favor and taken away my disgrace among the people.'" We see by these scriptures Elizabeth is quite aware that Zechariah and the entire religious community blamed her for her barrenness, her "disgrace." She is a righteous woman, living with a "blameless" man, and still she is in disgrace. Until that moment, she does not realize her barrenness is all a part of God's plan to "prepare the way for the Lord."

When Mary arrives to visit, Elizabeth is six months' pregnant. Women can usually tell when another woman is pregnant, but Elizabeth perceives something much greater. When she sees Mary, the scripture says Elizabeth is "filled with the Holy Spirit" and is given a revelation. She knows Mary is pregnant with the Messiah. She doesn't question it. She doesn't know how this came to be, but she recognizes God's hand in it.

Elizabeth had prayed a long time for a child. For years the great desire of her heart was unfulfilled. Nevertheless, she remains faithful to God. When she least expects it, suddenly God chooses her to carry out his plan for mankind's redemption. Her son will be instrumental in pointing the way to the Messiah.

In Luke 1:42-45, Elizabeth sees Mary approaching. When the young woman is close enough to shout a greeting, Elizabeth is filled with the Holy Spirit and speaks.

> "In a loud voice she exclaimed: 'Blessed are you among women, and blessed is the child you will bear! But why am I so favored, that the mother of my Lord should come to me? As soon as the sound of your greeting reached my ears, the baby in my womb leaped for joy. Blessed is she who has believed the Lord would fulfill his promises to her.'"

Through the power of the Holy Spirit, Elizabeth confirms Mary is carrying the Messiah. How else could she know? She is given a word of knowledge from God. She receives a revelation. She speaks with conviction what God has revealed to her. There is no other way she could know that Mary's pregnancy is the fulfillment of God's promise. She recognizes instantly that God has favored them both. When she hears Mary's greeting her unborn child stirs in her womb with such power she senses he is leaping with joy.

Her joyful welcome must have soothed Mary's heart and eased her anxiety. Mary probably heard of the miracle of Elizabeth's pregnancy and this may be why she chose to travel a fair distance to her cousin's house. This touching moment when the two women greet each other, recognizing God's hand in each other's lives, is an example to all godly women to encourage and support one another. If God chooses to work through a certain woman, it is vital that she receive encouragement from the women around her. Jealousy and competitiveness have no place in God's family.

It is good to note that as much as Elizabeth and Mary share in common, they are not alike. One is old, the other young. One has prestige and position as the wife of a priest, the other is nobody special, and yet God brings them together to comfort and encourage one another. Because Mary stays with her for quite awhile, we can assume Elizabeth enjoys her company. There is so much to talk about, even though at this point she doesn't know all that transpired between her husband and the archangel.

It isn't until her son is born and officially named that her husband is able to verbally reveal Gabriel's prophesy about their son and the coming Messiah. The Holy Spirit has already given Elizabeth supernatural knowledge upon Mary's arrival. There is an instant bond between the much older woman and her young cousin. The two become extremely close and Mary stays with Elizabeth for three months, which means she probably helped with the birth of John. Imagine these two women, one an old married woman and the other a young virgin, neither of whom have experienced giving birth, helping and encouraging one another. It is quite possible that Mary learned much from this birth, preparing her for what was to come.

I was seventeen when I conceived my firstborn son; I had never held an infant before he was put into my arms at the hospital. I remember I could not wait to unwrap this little bundle and look at his ten fingers and toes. I was in awe of what had come out of my body. I was so happy! The nurse came in and shouted at me "What have you done! Now I will have to wrap him up again!" She snatched him from my arms and took him away. I did not dare examine him again until we took him home three days later. I was so young, so scared. I had no idea what to do with an infant. I empathize so much with young Mary of Nazareth and wish I had had an Elizabeth to go to for advice and support.

My family was quite upset with me. All their grand plans for me were dashed in a moment when they found out I was pregnant. The depth of their disappointment and shame affected me for many years. They were right. I was too young. I was not ready to be a mother, but my children did not overly suffer from my ignorance and naiveté.

However, from my experience as a young mother, I learned how important it is for a young woman to have an older woman to guide her. More than likely, it is not her mother. In fact, the mother is often the last person a girl will go to for advice and certainly Mary did not go to her mother. She went to an older cousin, a woman who lived a considerable distance away.

I did not understand my own mother's immediate reaction to my teenage pregnancy. I thought she would be happy — a new life was growing inside of me. I didn't know as she did how children can "pierce the heart." The mother's way is a painful, lonely way. Though our bodies can conceive as early as age twelve, we are not mature enough to absorb all the shocks of motherhood until we are much older. I am not putting down young motherhood, but I also find it disingenuous to glamorize the situation as if it were without cost. Older, wiser women owe it to themselves and to younger women to be candid, frank and open on the tender subjects of sex, conception, and motherhood. We each need to trust ourselves to pass on our woman's wisdom.

Elizabeth is a wise and godly woman. Everything known about Elizabeth is rooted in an Old Testament covenant relationship with God. Whereas young Mary has absolutely nothing obvious to recommend her as the chosen vessel for the Messiah — representing the New Covenant — Elizabeth is the epitome of Old Testament righteousness and service, with impressive credentials and lineage going back to the brother of Moses and the first High Priest of the Israelites to dispense Mosaic Law under the Old Covenant. There can be no doubt of Elizabeth's pedigree. If anyone should logically give birth to the Messiah, it would have been Elizabeth. She is the only woman in the New Testament who is given the designation "righteous."

Luke 1:6 states, "Both of them [Zechariah and Elizabeth] were righteous in the sight of God, observing all the Lord's commands and decrees blamelessly." In the Old Testament, a righteous person is one who carefully observes Mosaic Law. Surely, a righteous, blameless, credentialed Jewish woman of God is the perfect choice to bring the Messiah into the world. But no, something new and amazing is happening at this time. Although Mary is of the line of David, she is the young, unmerited, innocent one of the New Covenant, which supersedes the perfect, blameless, righteous woman of the Old Covenant.

When Mary (New Covenant) races to meet Elizabeth (Old Covenant) and they greet one another, the women both experience great joy. John the Baptist "leaps" within his mother's womb at the mere presence of the embryonic Jesus in Mary's womb. This combining of Old and New Covenant is a joyous moment unlike any other recorded in the scriptures.

Elizabeth immediately blesses Mary and validates the secret in Mary's heart — she carries the Messiah in fulfillment of Old Testament prophecies. Mary's presence also validates Elizabeth's secret that the child in her own womb will be as Elijah, who will "make ready a people prepared for the Lord" (Luke 1:17). Each supports the other. It gives further credence that the Old Testament points the way to God's plan for the salvation of his Creation through the Messiah.

It also should be noted that although the archangel Gabriel visits Mary, Elizabeth has no such visitation. God deals differently with her. It is Elizabeth's husband who is visited by the supernatural being. When Zechariah returns home, unable to share this remarkable revelation, Elizabeth must take it on faith. To her, the miracle of her own pregnancy is all the confirmation she needs.

She is an old, barren woman, righteous and patient, awaiting the blessing of God in the face of mounting evidence God has abandoned her. A woman past her fertile prime is unlikely to get pregnant. Did Elizabeth waver? Did she doubt? I imagine Elizabeth had moments of feeling God's favor was not upon her, but because she is called "righteous and blameless," I believe she has faith that somehow, at some time, God will hear her prayer and give her a child — as he had Sarah, Rachel, and Hannah.

Both Mary and Elizabeth become integral to the salvation of humanity.

These once seemingly insignificant women become players on a stage with worldwide and eternal ramifications. They both are filled with the Holy Spirit. They both prophesy. They both are made aware of God's plan before it is made public.

~ ~ ~ ~ ~

MEDITATION

The story of Elizabeth illuminates a transition between the Old and New Covenants. Because we live under the New Covenant, the Lord has brought us grace and freedom through the atonement of Jesus Christ. Ask the Lord to show you where you may be operating under Old Covenant law and how to appropriate his New Covenant promises.

Elizabeth had faith well into her old age that she would receive the favor of God to bear a child. Is there something for which you are waiting on God yet to be fulfilled? Meditate on Elizabeth's story so that you may be strengthened as you await the fulfillment of God's promise.

For the word of the Lord is right and true; He is faithful in all He does. — Psalms 33:4

He has made us competent as ministers of a new covenant — not of the letter but of the Spirit; for the letter kills, but the Spirit gives life. — 2 Corinthians 3:6

Study Guide Questions

ELIZABETH

— List three things you want to remember about Elizabeth.

— Why is Elizabeth significant? Why did God choose her?

— What does Elizabeth's story tell you about the faithfulness of God?

— Do you find women are often competitive with each other? How does this story encourage you to be more supportive of other women?

— Discuss what it means that Elizabeth is of the Old Covenant and Mary is of the New Covenant.

— Do you have a relationship with an older female relative or a friend? How does this friendship support your walk with God?

— What can you do to mentor and encourage younger women in the faith? Do you know anyone who may need your guidance? What practical steps can you take to become more accessible to her?

NOTES

IV

PROPHET ANNA

According to the Gospel of Luke, Anna is a known prophet who lives in Jerusalem. Luke has no problem saying she is "a prophet." This indicates she makes many prophecies, not just the one time when she sees Jesus, who is probably less than two months old. Their lives intersect when his parents enter the courts of the temple to present him to the Lord as required by the Law.

> "There was also a prophet, Anna, the daughter of Penuel, of the tribe of Asher. She was very old; she had lived with her husband seven years after her marriage, and then was a widow until she was eighty-four. She never left the temple but worshiped night and day, fasting and praying. Coming up to them at that very moment, she gave thanks to God and spoke about the child to all who were looking forward to the redemption of Jerusalem."
> — Luke 2:26-38

Anna is the proverbial wise woman who despite her gender and advanced age is used by God to reveal the advent of the Messiah. Within a rigid, male-centered culture, she contradicts the tradition that older women have little or no importance. She is called by name. She comes to our attention through two verses in Luke bringing us a wealth of information about women's role, power, and importance to God.

She is mentioned because God wants us to know he sanctifies women as well as men. God uses women as well as men. God speaks through women as well as men. God brings revelation to women as well as men. God rewards a woman's faithfulness as much as any man's. Women are blessed because of Anna, and I thank God for her inclusion in the Gospels.

Since her mention in the scriptures comes directly after the Holy Family's encounter with a righteous, devout man named Simeon in the temple courts, it is likely Anna is standing in either the Court of Gentiles or the Court of Women since those are the only two places a woman was allowed to be.

The passages regarding Simeon should be enough to confirm someone other than Mary and Joseph recognize the Messiah (even though Jesus is an infant), but Luke also includes the story of Anna's encounter with Jesus. Why? It is not only important to add emphasis on the collaboration of two witnesses, but from these two scriptures we see so much about how God loves and recognizes women, especially elderly women.

In verse 36, we learn much about Anna. First, she is a prophet. She is acknowledged in the scriptures as a woman who hears from God. Although the majority of prophets in the Bible are male, there are references to a few female prophets. God truly does not play favorites. He speaks to and through women as well as men. Some other Old Testament female prophets are Miriam (Exodus 15:20), Deborah (Judges 4:4), Abigail (1 Samuel 25:23-35), Huldah (2 Kings 22:14), and Isaiah's wife (Isaiah 8:3).

Anna is the first woman named as a prophet in the New Testament. After Jesus' death and resurrection, when the gift of the Holy Spirit has been imparted to the disciples at Pentecost, many women received the gift of prophecy. A prophet is called by God and speaks for him through the Holy Spirit. They are given the gift of foreknowledge. Anna is acknowledged as one who hears from God and has the authority to speak God's words.

Because Luke reveals her name, as well as her family line, it is likely she is well known and respected by the people of her time. She is designated by her Greek name, Anna, but in Hebrew, it is Hannah, which means grace or gift.[5] When she comes face-to-face with Jesus she prophesies that the child she sees will bring redemption to Jerusalem — redemption through grace. I am continually amazed by the illumination of the small details in the Bible. The manifestation of the gift of God's grace — the infant Jesus — is revealed to a woman of God whose Hebrew name means grace.

Why is she known by her Greek name and not her Hebrew name? Perhaps her husband of seven years is a Greek and she takes on the Greek name, but because the scripture also indicates her Jewish family line there can be no doubt that she is a daughter of Israel. By calling her Anna, Luke lets us know she is both a Gentile and a Jew — representing the whole of humanity.

She is the daughter of Penuel of the tribe of Asher, one of the twelve tribes of Israel dispersed during the first exile. When they return to Israel they settle in a region north of Jerusalem.[6] Because Anna now resides in Jerusalem, this reference to her family line also indicates that although once dispersed, she and members of her tribe have returned to the Holy City as promised by God (Genesis 50:24-25). She represents the redemption of God's promise, which is reinforced by the fact that she is given the gift of actually seeing the Messiah who brings redemption to the whole world.

We learn she is quite old. In fact, the scripture states she is 84, a surprising age for the time. Is there significance in indicating her age? In ancient Judaism and early Christianity, numbers were significant and often represented more than a quantitative measurement. They had symbolic meaning.

Anna's age comprises seven twelves. In sacred Scriptures, seven represents completion or spiritual perfection; it can also represent the covenant between God and man. The number twelve most often represents perfect order, divine government or the fulfillment of the law, which you can see with the twelve tribes of Israel, the twelve Apostles, twelve months of the year, etc.

When the number seven is added to the one and the two (1+2) it equals ten. Ten relates to human governments and law. When you add the numbers in her age, eight and four (8+4) it equals twelve. Eight represents new beginnings and four represents God's creation.[7] Luke may have revealed Anna's age for its symbolic meaning.

The scripture noting Anna's age is one of the few passages in the New Testament referring to a person's years. Why is mentioning her age so important? If she was between 12 and 15 years old when she married and her husband died seven years later when she is 19 or 22, she is a young woman when she is widowed. Because this passage is somewhat ambiguous, it is not clear how old Anna actually is. Most believe she is 84, but some interpretations put her age at over 100, calculating her age from the time she is widowed, likely in her twenties, and adding 84 years. Whichever interpretation one follows, Luke makes it clear Anna is quite elderly.

The beauty of Anna's age is not that she survives so long, but that even at her advanced age she has a purpose and an important role to play in God's plan. God is not finished with Anna yet. God gives her long life so he can reward her faithfulness by coming face-to-face with the hope of salvation through Jesus Christ. This is important to understand because often in church life today, older women are relegated to "hospitality" or "child care" duties. Even after years of service to God, their wisdom may be discounted or ignored and they are not considered for leadership roles in the congregation.

I know several very godly women in their eighties. The knowledge and wisdom they have is a storehouse of treasure. Unfortunately, the church often gives poor attention to these elderly women (except for indulgent lip service) and thus misses sharing their spiritual gold.

My own mother is in her nineties. She has been guiding my spiritual life since before I became a Christian. Whenever I am in need of powerful prayer, I call my mother. She is a devoted Christian, a widow, and God has blessed her with long life and a lively mind. At her age, she has said she often feels left out and ignored at church because the advancing years take a toll on the body and mind. There are few opportunities for her to minister in the church as she did in her earlier years because the emphasis is placed on men and young families to the exclusion of wise older women.

Churches can benefit by eagerly seeking the talents and spiritual insights elderly women offer. According to Proverbs 14:1a, "a wise woman builds up her house," or as we could say, "A wise woman builds up the church."

The message from Anna's distinction in the Gospel of Luke is God honors, respects, and rewards older women, particularly widows.[8] He orchestrates the arrival of the Holy Family at a time when Anna is in the courtyard of the Temple, and within earshot of Simeon. We do not know exactly where Anna is on the Temple grounds. The Court of Gentiles includes a bazaar full of vendors where people can purchase sacrificial animals, buy food and drink, and exchange money. Anyone can have access to this court. It would be a noisy, bustling place full of people and animals.

The Court of Women is the largest of the courts and is open only to Jewish men and women. More than likely, Anna is there but it is a noisy, busy place full of talking, shouting, dancing, and singing. In this chaos old Anna overhears Simeon speaking privately to Mary. What are the chances she is in the exact place at the exact time to encounter the Christ child? It is a miracle for Anna to be "coming up to them at that very moment." This clearly demonstrates God hears and answers the intercessory prayers of older women. Anna dispels all notions that such women have no role to play in the Kingdom of God. In this instance, Anna is not only an intercessor; she is a prophet.

Let us talk about what Anna is doing. The scripture says she "never left the temple but worshiped day and night, fasting and praying" (Luke 2:37b). God responded to Anna's prayers. She is a woman of great faith and devotion. Because she became a widow at such a young age, it is surprising she did not remarry. We can speculate either she had no offers of marriage or she decided to dedicate her life to God. I believe Anna chose to devote her time and attention in service to God — she had a holy calling.

There is no reference to any male relative taking care of Anna. As far as we can determine, she is completely alone, and for a woman to be childless and a widow, it is unusual that she is not under the protection of a man. How has she survived so long? She is under the protection of God and is honored due to her age. Throughout the Bible, God commands his people to take special care of the widows and orphans. Anna may have received some kind of widow's compensation from local synagogues or the temple since it appears she lived there.

Most likely, Anna is a Nazirite (Numbers 6:1-8), a person who has taken a vow to separate from others for service to God. The Nazirite vow, for both men and women, includes abstaining from the fruit of the vine (wine, grapes, raisins, vinegar), never cutting one's hair, and avoiding corpses or graves.

Staying on the temple grounds, day and night, Anna is assured she will not be exposed to these. She would have access to the Court of Gentiles for food and drink. In addition, she will have long, long hair. We cannot even imagine how long her hair was. It is possible this was one of the reasons everyone knew about Anna. An eighty-four-year-old woman with long, long hair, who is in a constant state of worship (possibly singing, shouting or prophesying), would be something to see.

There is another godly Christian woman in my life who is 84. Her name is Katherine. Not unlike Anna, she could be considered a Nazirite since she has dedicated her entire life in service to Christ.

She never married, even though she is attractive and probably received many offers. Her hair is short and pure white; her body is slightly bent, and she uses a cane. Talking to Katherine is like coming into a storeroom of gold and being showered with gold dust. The depth of her spirit and the maturity of her devotion is a rare gift. When she speaks, she brings revelation to the scriptures from decades of study and prayer. She uses a cane because she has spent the greater part of her life on her knees before God. Fortunately for Katherine, she attends a church that greatly honors her and seeks her wisdom. How many other churches understand the importance of spiritually wise old women?

Anna is an intercessor. She prays and fasts day and night for the redemption of her people. Even though she is old, her body emaciated and she is probably suffering the typical ailments of old age, she maintains her life's purpose — to intercede for her people. As a woman, according to Old Covenant law, she is not able to serve in an official priestly role, (she is not able to offer sacrifices), but she is a priest nonetheless.

We can learn from Anna's example. As a child of God, we women serve in a royal priesthood: "But you are a chosen people, a royal priesthood, a holy nation, God's special possession, that you may declare the praises of him who called you out of darkness into his wonderful light" (1 Peter 2:9).

She is also an evangelist. Upon seeing Jesus, the scriptures say she "spoke about the child to all" (Luke 2:38). She knew immediately, by divine revelation, that this little baby was the promised Messiah. She is gifted with this revelation.

We can surmise this is Anna's fervent prayerful entreaty. Once the Christ child is revealed to her, she tells everyone what she knows: "Fear not! The Messiah has come! I have seen him with my own eyes! You who hope in the redemption of Jerusalem praise God for he has been faithful! His promises endure forever! Hallelujah!"

~ ~ ~ ~ ~

MEDITATION

What has God called you to do? What is your destiny? You can choose to follow it or not. God does not force his will on his daughters. If you are eager to find your divine path and walk in his footsteps, meditate on Anna and how she followed her path without receiving any confirmation until late in her life. It was grander than anything she could have expected.

God's ways are true and right. If we are faithful, he is abundantly faithful. Believe God knows you well, daughter, and wants to give you the desires of your heart as he gave Anna her heart's desire.

Direct my footsteps according to your word; let no sin rule over me. — Psalms 119:133

Since my youth, God, you have taught me, and to this day I declare your marvelous deeds. Even when I am old and gray, do not forsake me, my God, till I declare your power to the next generation, your mighty acts to all who are to come. — Psalms 71:17-18

Study Guide Questions

PROPHET ANNA

— List three things you want to remember about Prophet Anna.

— From this story, do you have a better understanding of God's use of women as prophets and evangelists? What does it mean to be a prophet or evangelist? How does this translate to today?

— What does this story say about God's promises and faithfulness? Explain.

— Do you think older women in the church are respected and valued for their wisdom? Give an example. If not, how can you help to change this?

— Do you know a "wise woman/prophet?" Can you reach out to her and let her know you value her? What are some of the ways you can honor her?

— What practical steps can you take to bring more recognition to older, more spiritually mature women in your church or group? List three things that could be implemented.

NOTES

V

LITTLE DAUGHTER

"Now when Jesus returned, a crowd welcomed him, for
they were all expecting him. Then a man named Jairus, a
synagogue leader, came and fell at Jesus's feet, pleading
with him to come to his house because his only daughter,
a girl of about twelve, was dying." — Luke 8:40-42a

An entire crowd witnesses the resurrection miracle of Jairus' little
daughter. The story contains a great amount of detail, but gives little
information about the little girl, other than she is almost twelve years old.

The Gospels of Matthew, Mark, and Luke record Jesus' face-to-face
encounter with this young girl. The Gospel of John does not; however,
John states at the end of his Gospel, "Jesus did many other things as
well. If every one of them were written down, I suppose that even the
whole world would not have room for the books that would be written"
(John 21:25).

However, John is one of the Twelve who went into the girl's house and witnessed the miracle. There is no way of knowing why he did not include this amazing event in his account of Jesus' life. Perhaps it is because Jesus told them not to say anything.

This encounter with Jesus centers almost exclusively on Jairus, the little girl's father. Because the little girl is not named and does not speak, we can deduce she is another nameless, faceless, and essentially mute female in Jesus' time. Upon careful reading and meditation, we find within this encounter a tremendous truth for women.

This is a story of a father's love for his little girl.

All three Gospel accounts combine two distinctive stories. From the time Jairus comes to Jesus until his young daughter's miraculous healing, the story is bisected by the miracle of the bleeding woman. Most commentaries combine these two miraculous events because of their striking similarities and distinct contrasts. I will address them separately to reveal the singular interaction of Jesus with these two females who play a significant role in his ministry regarding women.

Almost as soon as Jairus appears to ask for help for his dying little girl, Jesus is interrupted by a woman with a medical problem and stops to have a personal encounter with her. The story of Jairus' daughter continues in Luke 8:49-56:

> "While Jesus was still speaking, someone came from the house of Jairus, the synagogue leader. 'Your daughter is dead,' he said. 'Don't bother the teacher anymore.'
>
> Hearing this, Jesus said to Jairus, 'Don't be afraid; just believe, and she will be healed.' When he arrived at the house of Jairus, he did not let anyone go in with him except Peter, John and James, and the child's father and mother.

Meanwhile, all the people were wailing and mourning for her. 'Stop wailing,' Jesus said. 'She is not dead but asleep.' They laughed at him, knowing she was dead. But he took her by the hand and said, 'My child, get up!' Her spirit returned, and at once she stood up. Then Jesus told them to give her something to eat. Her parents were astonished, but he ordered them not to tell anyone what had happened."

The first thing we notice is Jesus is in the middle of a large crowd, but the people make way for Jairus because he is a well-known leader in the synagogue. He falls at Jesus' feet, begging for his daughter's life. This must have shocked those around him. To humble oneself like this is a sign of great humility from the petitioner and shows great deference for the other.

His action focuses all attention on Jesus. Imagine how the crowd falls silent in stunned surprise. They hear Jairus' plea, which I cannot imagine is conveyed in a soft voice. He probably speaks in a loud voice to be certain Jesus can hear him. Everyone waits with bated breath to see what Jesus will say and what he will do.

If a known synagogue leader can prostrate himself in front of Jesus and beg for a miracle, this action would have brought even greater credibility to Jesus' ministry. It says much about Jairus. His action demonstrates his desperation and his great love for his daughter. He does not care how it looks, who sees him, or what it will do to his reputation; he has one last hope that this man Jesus, who has healed others, will heal his critically ill daughter.

Matthew's account has it that Jairus' daughter is already dead and he asks Jesus to bring her back to life. If this is the more accurate picture, then we must see Jairus either as one who is out of his mind with grief and cannot accept his daughter's death, or one who has already fully accepted Jesus as the Messiah. If we follow Luke's account, the little girl is close to death and no one can save her.

The scripture says she is his only daughter. It does not say she is his only child, so Jairus may have sons. At the time, sons are highly valued and daughters are valued only for their bride price or for making a profitable alliance. Perhaps the loss of his daughter will mean the loss of monetary gain. However, given his actions, we surmise that Jairus deeply loves his daughter. She is the apple of his eye. He is willing to sacrifice his honor in the midst of a crowd in a culture that operates by honor-shame customs.

We also learn she is twelve years old. As we have stated before, young girls are considered marriageable from as early as 12 to 15 years old. This little girl will have been entering the age when she will start her menses, and, therefore, be able to marry and conceive. However, in all accounts, she is considered a child rather than a marriageable woman. In Mark, Jesus calls her "little girl," in Luke she is "child" and in Matthew, she is "girl." Everyone appears to agree that she is still a child.

Because he is a religious leader, Jairus is not a poor man. He would be considered wealthy, or at least well off, and we can imagine he lavishes his wealth on his only daughter. She lacks for nothing — nothing but health. For all his prosperity and prestige, Jairus is helpless. He cannot save her. He probably brought in physicians when she did not get any better. Because of his love for her, we can imagine every physician in Jerusalem has seen her. Now she is at the point of death. No one can save her — no one but Jesus.

With a synagogue leader at his feet and the crowd pressing all around, gawking and whispering at the scene, Jesus has compassion for the man because the scripture states he goes with him right away. But then the bleeding woman appears and delays Jesus' progress.

The delay appears to have cost precious seconds between life and death. Messengers arrive and tell Jairus his daughter is dead and not to bother the rabbi any longer. You can imagine him tearing his cloak, dropping to his knees and pouring dust on his head; but the scriptures say Jesus hears the messengers and speaks immediately to Jairus, saying, "Do not be afraid, just believe and she will be healed."

Obviously, Jairus believes because they continue on to his house. The whole crowd follows to see what will happen: Jairus running like a madman toward his home, Jesus running after him, his disciples running to keep up, and the crowd running after them all.

When they arrive, they find a cacophony of wailing. Jairus is an influential man. Everyone who wants to be in his good graces tries to show respect by their impressive wails of grief — there will be the child's mother, relatives, friends, colleagues and the curious, and possibly paid mourners who will be wailing and crying about the death of this little girl.

The little girl's mother might see Jairus coming and fall into his arms, overcome with grief. But Jesus takes control of the situation immediately. Luke 8:51 says, "He did not let anyone go in with him except Peter, John and James, and the child's father and mother."

I love that Jesus includes the little girl's mother in this exclusive gathering. Not that he could have restrained her. There is nothing so fierce as a mother's love for her child. I can imagine her barging in no matter what it cost her in status and honor. She does not have to do this because Jesus invites her.

They go into the room where the little girl lies on her bed. She looks so peaceful. She could be sleeping, except for the stillness, and the grief etched on the faces of her parents. There can be no doubt she is dead. They are in so much pain.

I can see them standing there, clinging to each other, desperate for a miracle. I think the mother's faith is one of the reasons Jesus invites her in. She might have been the one who demanded her husband seek out the healer Jesus. Because of their faith, Jesus is able to perform the miracle they seek.

I imagine at this point Jesus feels some exasperation. There is too much noise. People are carrying on and making such a ruckus he cannot be heard. He shouts at them, "Stop wailing! She is not dead but asleep!" Did he go to a window and shout this? Did he go to the door? We do not know, but we know even though they are making a lot of noise, the crowd hears him because, "They laughed at him, knowing that she was dead."

This is a startling statement — from wailing and rending of clothes to derisive laughter. It shows how insensitive and uncaring these people are, what their motives really are. Their mourning is superficial at best and hypocritical at worst. They are there for themselves, not for Jairus, his wife, or their daughter. Jesus can always see the condition of people's hearts.

He returns to the girl's bedside and takes her lifeless hand in his. "My child, get up!" Notice he does not pray a long, involved prayer. He does not rebuke and bind death. He merely commands her to get up.

The scriptures state at this point "her spirit returned and she stood up." Then he gives her parents some practical advice. He tells them to feed her. In other words, she is completely restored to life. She can get up, she can walk, and she can eat like any normal child. Her parents are astonished.

Then Jesus tells them not to tell anyone what has happened. This is curious. Don't you think when all those people saw Jairus' daughter walking, talking, and playing outside they would know something has happened? She was dead and is now alive! How were they to keep this miracle quiet?

Is Jesus joking? No. He knows word of this child's resurrection will spread like wildfire. He does not want Jairus and his wife to be put in the position of trying to explain what happened. He does not want the story to outweigh the reality. The miracle is enough. The details are unimportant. What is important is their little girl was dead and is now alive. She has been fully restored to her parents.

I had a special, loving relationship with my father. I was the first girl born after two boys and my father fell in love with me instantly. As I grew, he was a strong presence in my life. I have many endearing memories of how he watched over me, guided me, and encouraged me to reach my potential. He never let me feel like I was less of a human being than my brothers.

However, to be honest, in the beginning he did have some misguided cultural notions about what a girl could and could not do. There were masculine tasks and feminine tasks — painting the house and mowing the lawn were masculine tasks; setting the table and cleaning the house were feminine tasks. I, on the other hand, only wanted to mow the lawn and paint the house.

At the age of six I began to push back against male-female stereotypes. And my father could not have been prouder. His love for me gave me the freedom to be all I could be. Once he realized I was as capable as my brothers to tackle certain tasks, and I actually wanted to do these things, he stepped aside and allowed me to fly.

Fathers can make such an impact on their little daughters. A father who truly loves his daughter will guide and protect her, but never stifle or deny her destiny. This particular encounter reveals how much the Lord values little girls. He went out of his way to bring a little girl back from the dead because of the love demonstrated by her father.

This is why it is so important for the church to encourage women to fulfill their divine calling, whether as a teacher, evangelist, hostess, guide, prophet, apostle, pastor, priest or healer. This is how the church itself will find its full power.

The story of Jairus is about a father's love for his daughter. Jesus saw in Jairus a perfect example of the Father's love for his children. He wants us all to know the Father's love for his little girls. Your life is important.

Jairus suffered pain and humiliation as he lay in the dust at Jesus' feet in the hope of saving his daughter's life. Jesus suffered humiliation and pain for you and laid down his life for you so you may have your life restored — and even more.

> "For God so loved the world that He gave His one and only Son, that whoever believes in Him shall not perish but have eternal life." — John 3:16

This is a story of God's love for you, little daughter.

~ ~ ~ ~ ~

MEDITATION

This spiritual exercise may be more difficult than you expect, but it will expand your relationship with the Lord. Meditate on God as your Daddy (*Abba*). The word *Abba* is an Aramaic word, which most closely translates as the familiar "Daddy." It indicates a close, intimate relationship between a father and his child. Imagine yourself as God's little daughter.

Now lie back and imagine you are in the arms of the Lord. Feel his arms around you. Feel the hug he is giving to you. Relax. Enjoy being on his lap and in his arms. Completely surrender to his great love for you. Allow yourself to be loved. He is your Daddy (*Abba Father*) and he thinks you are amazing, precious and loveable. Let go of your fears and worries.

You are in his arms now.

Because you are his sons [daughters], God sent the Spirit of his Son into our hearts, the Spirit who calls out, "Abba, Father." — *Galatians 4:6*

And "I will be a Father to you, and you will be my sons and daughters, says the Lord Almighty." — *2 Corinthians 6:18*

Study Guide Questions

LITTLE DAUGHTER

— List three things you want to remember about Little Daughter.

— Who is the little girl's father? Why is he significant?

— What motivated Jesus to go with Jairus? What motivated the "mourners?"

— This is one of three miraculous resurrection stories recorded in the Gospels. Why is it noteworthy one of them is a little girl? Explain your answer.

— Imagine how you would react if you were the parents and Jesus said your daughter was alive? Explain how this story increases your faith?

— Why do you think Jesus told the parents not to say anything? Is there a time to share what God has done in your life and a time to keep quiet about it? How do you know the difference?

— What does this story say about the Father's love for his daughters?

NOTES

VI

BLEEDING WOMAN

Within the story of Jairus' little daughter is the miraculous story of the woman whose body is healed of excessive bleeding. This story has been told time and time again because it is so powerful. It is also particular to women. No man can understand this woman as other women can. Men do not bleed every month. Women do.

From puberty to menopause, a woman is captive to her monthly period. It affects her life, from the fear and awe of her first monthly flow to the sorrow and freedom of her last. Women bleed once a month and yet do not die. This is fundamentally female; to some extent women plan their lives around their menses.

This story is deeply personal and poignant from a female perspective. As women, this story perhaps is more personal in our eyes than any other. In the midst of a great crowd of men, one sick, vulnerable woman stops Jesus in his tracks. What makes this encounter so unusual is Jesus does not initiate it and no one else does either. There are no male relatives, no father, brother, or husband to bring this woman's plight to the attention of the Healer. On her own, and in defiance of Judaic Law, the hemorrhaging woman seeks out Jesus for her healing.

There are three accounts of this healing. The Gospels of Matthew, Mark, and Luke all record it and by reading all three we gain a more complete picture of what happens. Matthew's account (Matthew 9:20-22) is told in three verses. Mark's account (Mark 5:25-34) is the longest, told in ten verses, and gives us the best picture of the woman's circumstances. Luke's account (Luke 8:43-48), written in six verses, affirms the other two reports.

Here is the account written in Matthew:

> "Just then a woman who had been subject to bleeding for twelve years came up behind him and touched the edge of his cloak. She said to herself, 'If I only touch his cloak, I will be healed.' Jesus turned and saw her. 'Take heart, daughter,' he said, 'your faith has healed you.' And the woman was healed from that moment."

What we learn from these verses, which is repeated in the other two Gospels, is a woman suffers from a bleeding disorder (most likely involving her reproductive organs) for twelve years. She seeks Jesus out by herself. She believes if she touches his clothes, she will be healed. Jesus sees her and speaks to her. He declares it is by her faith she is healed. He calls her "daughter." And she is instantly healed.

According to the Law of Moses, any woman with a discharge of blood is unclean. Chapter 15 of the Book of Leviticus outlines what is considered "clean" and "unclean." Since women menstruate monthly, women are unclean on a regular basis.

In verse 19, women are unclean for seven days during their menses and anyone who touches them during this time will be fouled. This means for one week out of every month, women are excluded from society. This seems particularly harsh treatment for women, who, after all, have no control over the natural functions of their bodies. When I first read about this, I was outraged.

If this also makes your blood boil, so to speak, then Leviticus 12:2 and Leviticus 12:5 will make it even worse. These scriptures offer further evidence of the extreme harshness of Judaic Law toward women. According to these scriptures, if a woman gives birth to a son, she is unclean for seven days; but if she gives birth to a daughter, she is unclean for fourteen days and has to continue ritual purification or *mikvah* for sixty-six days.

Does this appear profoundly unfair to women? What does it say about how the Lord views us? When I first read this, it hurt me to think God thought so poorly of us he actually punished us for being born female. Was this proof that my existence as a female made me less human in the eyes of my Creator?

I struggled with this for some time before I received a revelation there might be an underlying tenderness in its application for women. Instead of viewing it as a punishment, I began to see it as a blessing. During times of purification, onerous demands on women are lifted. By law they are separated from men, and, as a result, are free from the demands of the household. In her novel, *The Red Tent*, Anita Diamant [9] presents an engaging picture of what it was like for women of the Old Testament. She brings a new perspective to the stigma of being temporarily impure or "unclean."

As for the unfairness of being ostracized for a longer period of time after giving birth to a daughter, in point of fact, it serves as a reprieve because wives will not have to endure the disappointment or wrath of their husbands for not having produced a son. To my mind, this extended period allows the husband something of an enforced "cooling off period" to adjust to his possible disappointment and allows the wife to recover before returning to her wifely duties. Although the Law appears harsh, it can also be seen as a Sovereign God's way of freeing women from their many tasks, at least for a little while.

Returning to the bleeding woman who seeks out Jesus, it must be noted the Law of Moses is still in effect. According to Leviticus 15:25, "When a woman has a discharge of blood for many days at a time other than her monthly period or has a discharge that continues beyond her period, she will be unclean as long as she has the discharge, just as in the days of her period."

Through the Mosaic Law, this poor woman has been ostracized as unclean for twelve long years. Because of this condition, she is not allowed to go out in public. And yet, hearing Jesus is nearby, she breaks the Law and goes out to find him, hoping against hope if she can only touch his clothes without him even knowing it, she will be healed of the disease that has made her a prisoner. In Mark's account (Mark 5:25-34), we learn more about the woman and how desperate she is:

"And a woman was there who had been subject to bleeding for twelve years. She had suffered a great deal under the care of many doctors and had spent all she had; yet instead of getting better she grew worse. When she heard about Jesus, she came up behind him in the crowd and touched his cloak, because she thought, 'If I just touch his clothes, I will be healed.'

Immediately her bleeding stopped and she felt in her body she was freed from her suffering. At once Jesus realized power had gone out from him. He turned around in the crowd and asked, 'Who touched my clothes?'

'You see the people crowding against you,' his disciples answered, 'and yet you can ask, 'Who touched me?' But Jesus kept looking around to see who had done it. Then the woman, knowing what had happened to her, came and fell at his feet and, trembling with fear, told him the whole truth.

> He said to her, 'Daughter, your faith has healed you. Go
> in peace and be freed from your suffering.'"

Not only is she suffering from an endless flow of blood, which must have made her extremely anemic, but she has "suffered a great deal under the care of many doctors and had spent all she had, yet instead of getting better, she grew worse" (v. 26). We can only imagine what kind of procedures she endured by the male physicians of that time. Whatever they did to her, she got worse. On top of that, she has spent all her money on their ineffectual treatments. In desperation, she takes matters into her own hands and enters the public streets to find the man she's heard about who heals all who come to him.

Mark 5:27 says she "came up behind him," and in a previous verse (Mark 5:24b), the scripture states "a large crowd followed and pressed around him." Imagine the scene: Jairus has fallen at Jesus' feet begging for his daughter's life, and Jesus has agreed to go with him to his house.

The crowd is completely caught up in this drama of the synagogue ruler's dying daughter and Jesus agreeing to help him. They do not want to be left out. They have to see the outcome. They are jostling each other to get to the front or stay there and are talking among themselves about what is happening. The woman sees her chance. Everyone's attention is fixed on Jairus and Jesus. No one will notice she is there.

She pushes her way through the crowd, not expecting any personal interaction with Jesus, but only hoping she can get close enough to touch his clothes. You can imagine she probably gets a few elbows in the face from those who do not want to give up their vantage point. Nevertheless, she presses on. There is so much desperation in her act.

Remember, she is probably anemic, weak from blood loss, maimed by the "treatment" of physicians, an outcast according to the Law of Moses, and without a penny to her name. She is without a doubt desperate, willing to be reviled, beaten or even killed if it means she may be freed from her uncontrollable bleeding. In Matthew's and Mark's accounts, we hear her inner voice. "If I only touch his cloak, I will be healed." Is it any wonder Jesus says to her, "Your faith has healed you."

With everything against her, she presses on. She pushes through the crowd and there he is, walking away from her. She can see his back. She reaches out her hand, straining to touch a piece of his cloak. Matthew and Luke state she "came up behind him and touched the edge of his cloak." According to both Mark and Luke, she is healed instantly. Mark states, "Immediately her bleeding stopped and she felt in her body that she was freed from her suffering" (v. 29). Luke concurs, "Immediately her bleeding stopped" (Luke 8:44b).

In both accounts, she is instantly aware something has happened in her body. For twelve years, she has suffered continual bleeding. She knows the instant the bleeding stops.

What is most amazing is we would know nothing about it if Jesus had not stopped and turned, asking, "Who touched me?" Everyone is following him, pushing each other to get near him, rushing towards Jairus' house, and a chronically sick woman reaches out her hand and touches his cloak, causing him to stop in his tracks. You can imagine how the crowd reacts. They stop, with those behind bumping into those in front. The whole group comes to a full stop as Jesus turns and asks a seemingly unimportant question. "Who touched me?"

Really? Who touched you, Jesus? What does he mean? In Mark, his disciples (more than likely right beside and behind him) ask the same question of him, reminding him that the crowd is large and any number of people might have touched his garment. They are confused, perplexed and possibly even afraid; thinking one of them might have inadvertently elbowed him.

In Luke's version of the story, Peter speaks for them all, "Master, the people are crowding and pressing against you." In other words, "Why are you asking? There is a crowd all around you?" It is so like Peter to state the obvious. After all this time, he is still baffled by the actions of Jesus.

There is something rather condescending about his words. He still sees Jesus as a great man, possibly the Messiah, but doubts he is a supernatural being, the Son of God and the Savior of all mankind. It is only after the Resurrection that Peter comes into the full awareness of who Jesus really is. We can certainly empathize with him. The reality of the situation; a large crowd pressing in, trying to be close to Jesus, will make it impossible to really know who touched him. The reality is not what we see with our eyes or can know by our natural senses. The reality is Jesus operates in the supernatural.

It is in Mark's account that we catch a glimpse of that supernatural walk: "At once Jesus realized that power had gone out from him" (v. 30). This surprising scripture reveals how sensitive to Shekinah Jesus is, how he walks continually in the supernatural. Even in the midst of a hurrying crowd, and with a separate mission in mind, power flows from him, activated by faith. The truth is there are probably others besides this one woman who have touched him during this episode, but her hand, reaching out in complete faith, activates the flow of the Holy Spirit.

Power is transmitted from Jesus' body into the woman's and she is healed instantly. In all the Gospels, this is the only time it is revealed that Jesus feels the outpouring of his supernatural power. What makes it so incredible is this power is transmitted not by the touching of flesh on flesh, but by flesh to mere cloth; the woman only touches the edge of his cloak. What makes the difference is not the method by which healing occurs but her simple act of faith.

Even though his disciples question him, scoffing at his sensitivity, and are eager to continue the journey to Jairus' house, Jesus stays put. The scripture states, "But Jesus kept looking around to see who had done it." Why does he stay put? If he knows power has gone from him, he also knows someone has received healing. Why does he stand his ground, looking to see who had touched him? Why did he put this woman through the humiliation of being publicly revealed? As the account continues, we learn why.

"Then the woman, knowing what had happened to her, came and fell at his feet and, trembling with fear, told him the whole truth" (v.33). Knowing what we know about Mosaic Law, we can understand why the woman trembles with fear. Knowing what we do about being female, we can understand how embarrassed she is to tell the "whole truth" in front of so many. But she cannot deny what has happened to her. For a dozen years she has suffered, and in an instant, she is miraculously healed. What must she have thought of Jesus, a man who can impart healing by a touch of his cloak?

Now he stops and is looking for her, asking, "Who touched me?" Her legs shake. She falls at his feet and confesses all, not knowing what will happen to her, extremely conscious of the fact she has defied the Law of Moses. From her trembling lips, Jairus, Peter, the disciples and the whole crowd learn that by the mere touch of Jesus' cloak, this poor, desperate, "unclean" woman is miraculously healed and Jesus knew exactly when it occurred.

When she finishes telling her story, of which we get this account in the three Gospels, Jesus says to her, "Daughter, your faith has healed you. Go in peace and be freed from your suffering" (v.34). He openly declares it is by her faith in him she receives her healing.

This is an important key to walking in the supernatural. It is by our faith in God that supernatural miracles occur in the physical realm. We do not deserve it. We have done nothing to earn it. We do not have to learn "magic words" or follow a prescribed method to manifest it. The only thing we have to do is to believe in the goodness of God and his desire to set us free from our infirmities. Our faith heals us. This is the great mystery. It is brought into the open by this beautiful story of a vulnerable, weak, penniless, suffering, "unclean" woman's faith in the Messiah.

However, there is another reason Jesus seeks out the one who touches him. He already knows she is healed, but before he moves on to Jairus' house, he wants to bless her over and above her physical healing. He says to her, "Go in peace and be freed from your suffering." He wants her and everyone there to know she is completely free; her ordeal is over. "Go in peace," he tells her.

I like to imagine at this point he takes her by the hand and pulls her to her feet. She can now stand and walk with her head up. She is no longer "unclean." Jesus imparts to her the peace of God, which passes all understanding. She is healed of her bleeding, but even beyond that, he tells her she is healed from her suffering. She had been deemed impure, ostracized by society, a prisoner in her house.

No more. She is free. She spent all her money on treatments and is penniless. No more. She has favor with God and her fortunes will be restored. The scriptures do not specifically state this, but we can take from Jesus' words to her he is imparting a greater blessing.

Perhaps the most beautiful and revealing word from Jesus in his encounter with this woman recorded in all three Gospels is he calls her "daughter." It is such an affectionate word of familiarity. Given that Jesus is in his early thirties and this woman has been suffering for more than twelve years, she is older than he is — and yet he calls her daughter.

Remember this story is embedded within the account of the healing of Jairus' daughter. In that story, we see the love of a father for his daughter; how he is willing to publicly humiliate himself on her behalf. Jesus is mindful of this. Jairus is right beside him. They are on their way to his house when this outcast woman's act of faith stops them all and she reveals the pain of her suffering and is miraculously healed.

She moves him. His words are as compassionate, intimate, loving and tender as a father's for his little girl. In this most feminine of stories, Jesus demonstrates we are his daughters and he loves us so much he is willing to abase himself on our behalf. As his daughters, we are free from the Law, healed of our suffering and blessed with his peace.

~ ~ ~ ~ ~

MEDITATION

Faith is the only thing required of us to activate the power of God. All is given to us — health, joy, prosperity, revelation, direction, wisdom — if only we activate our faith by declaring we believe in the Word of God.

Meditate on God's promises and then incorporate them into your life. You will begin to feel your belief as it rises within you, and as you take the steps of faith (even if your first few steps are shaky), God will have compassion on you and answer your prayer.

For the word of God is alive and active. Sharper than any double-edged sword, it penetrates even to dividing soul and spirit, joints and marrow; it judges the thoughts and attitudes of the heart. — *Hebrews 4:12*

But he was pierced for our transgressions, he was crushed for our iniquities; the punishment that brought us peace was on him, and by his wounds we are healed. — *Isaiah 53:5*

Study Guide Questions

BLEEDING WOMAN

— List three things you want to remember about the Bleeding Woman.

— This is a "female" story. Why do you think it is included in the scriptures?

— What does this story say about the way Jesus views female issues?

— Health issues can be challenging. How does this woman's faith and interaction with Jesus help you to address your own health concerns?

— What did Jesus mean when he says, "Daughter, your faith has healed you. Go in peace and be freed from your suffering." (v. 34)

— Is this woman courageous or simply desperate? Is she flouting the Law or fulfilling it? What does it say to you about exercising faith? Explain.

NOTES

VII

CRIPPLED WOMAN

The crippled woman's encounter with Jesus is one of those stories we might race by without really examining why Luke included it as one of the "many miracles" Jesus performed. We can learn much from this poor woman's plight and her transformation. Luke 13:10-13 recounts the episode:

> "On a Sabbath Jesus was teaching in one of the synagogues, and a woman was there who had been crippled by a spirit for eighteen years. She was bent over and could not straighten up at all. When Jesus saw her, he called her forward and said to her, 'Woman you are set free from your infirmity.' 'Then he put his hands on her, and immediately she straightened up and praised God.'"

What do we see from this encounter? Why does Luke include this healing from all the other miracles Jesus performed? What makes this example worth noting? The story of this healing reveals the heart of God. The healing of this crippled woman reveals the Kingdom of God.

Imagine the scene: There is a large crowd in the synagogue. Jesus is somewhere up front. The men will be there too — important men circling around Jesus, the synagogue ruler, the teachers, the prosperous merchants. The women will be sitting or standing to one side or at the back of the room, straining to hear, standing on their tiptoes to see. By this time, Jesus is a celebrity. Everyone wants to see and hear him, and many come to be healed. In this crowd is a woman who is "bent over and could not straighten up at all."

We cannot be certain what is wrong with her to cripple her so badly. She probably either has scoliosis or osteoporosis, a degenerative bone disease often afflicting women. According to the National Osteoporosis Foundation, 80 percent of the 10 million people who have the disease are women, and 55 percent of them are over age 50.[10] This is in today's world. Imagine how often this disease must have afflicted women 2,000 years ago. The leading cause of osteoporosis is a drop in estrogen.

This is not a modern day problem. This is a "woman's" problem. We can surmise she is probably at or beyond menopausal age. Osteoporosis occurs gradually in women. During menopause, due to the drop in estrogen, bone begins to crumble. This woman's vertebrae have collapsed, causing her spine to bend and double over. Even today, there is no cure for this disease. Prevention is the approach since deteriorated bone cannot be renewed.[11]

Jesus is teaching to a great crowd; men are pressing around him, women in the rear are straining to hear, and way in the back is a woman who is bent over. It is extremely painful for her to even stand there. Because of her condition, she probably has female relatives who bring her, guiding her to the synagogue painfully, step by step. It requires great determination and faith for her to come to the temple. She probably makes it a point to avoid crowds. A fall can prove fatal. Nevertheless, she perseveres and comes to the service to see Jesus with the hope she will be healed.

"When Jesus saw her, he called her forward" (v. 12). This is a beautiful scripture. Even though he is at the center of attention and all the important men are jostling each other to get close to him, he sees her and calls her forward.

In this vast universe, our Savior sees us — individually and personally and has compassion for us — women and men. How does he glimpse this little woman? Does the crowd part to let this crippled woman pass? Given that the culture had little regard for women and avoided people with diseases and infirmities, it is doubtful people made way for her to move closer to the Healer.

Is she a tall, imposing woman whose bearing brings attention? No, she is old, insignificant and bent over; she is probably half the height of a healthy woman. The crowd hides her from Jesus' view. How does he see her? He sees her through the Holy Spirit, *Shekinah*.

His spirit is drawn to her. His awareness of her is staggering. We know from scripture he "sees" supernaturally. In John 5:19, he says, "Very truly I tell you, the Son can do nothing by himself; he can do only what he sees his Father doing, because whatever the Father does the Son also does."

He sees what the Father reveals to him. However, he does not merely observe the disabled woman, he calls her forward. He makes the crowd part for her. He brings her from the back to the front; he brings her into the domain of men. He probably has the men step back so she can come right up to him. She stands before him — so close he can lay his hands on her.

Can you imagine how she feels, standing painfully in the back, maybe supported by her friends or family when Jesus calls her forward? We do not know exactly what he says, but it must have been something like, "You, the woman in the back who is bent over double, come to me."

She probably does not go out much. Not only is it too painful to walk, but she also has to endure unfriendly stares and mocking children. All eyes turn to her. She is used to people staring. In those days, one who is physically disabled is seen as either having committed a great sin or her parents sinned, causing her to be cursed. On top of her debilitating infirmity, she has to suffer the condemnation of the religious community. Even Luke states "a spirit" brings on her condition.

But Jesus does not cast out a demon or a spirit. He says, "Woman you are set free from your infirmity." Yes, all sickness comes from the devil, but it is a disease that has caused this woman's condition, not a demon. A disease that affects women happens to afflict her. Jesus calls it what it is, an infirmity — a physical weakness of the bone. "Then he put his hands on her, and immediately she straightened up and praised God" (v. 13).

First, he speaks, and then he lays his hands on her. As believers, we are called to lay our hands on the sick for their healing. In the Great Commission, after his resurrection, Jesus instructs believers in Mark 16:18 (KJV), "they [we] shall lay hands on the sick, and they shall recover." In this instance, Jesus declares her healed first and then places his hands on her.

Imagine this scene: The woman shuffles through the crowd toward the front of the temple, dreading the piercing eyes and looks of disgust on people's faces, and the indignation of the important men standing near Jesus, but she comes forward. She has the faith to be healed and is willing to endure public humiliation in the effort to reach Jesus.

So that everyone can hear, from the men near him to the women and the sick at the back, Jesus says, "Woman you are set free from your infirmity." Then he bends down and raises her up. In an instant, her back straightens — bone is regenerated and her spine is restored.

For eighteen years, this woman has been constrained to stare down at the ground and now she is looking into the face of Jesus. Can you imagine her surprise and joy? For the first time in all those years, she can look someone in the eye. And that someone is Jesus, the Son of God.

I try to imagine what his eyes looked like in this moment. I am sure they are full of love for this discarded, crippled woman. The scripture says her response to this was to praise God. She did not say, "thank you, rabbi." She praised God. She knew she had been touched miraculously by the power of God — Jesus, the Messiah, has touched her.

Jesus does not do anything halfway. Out of all the people who must have come to be healed, he selects this woman. Why? It is because he knows the people's hearts in that room. He wants to impart an important truth to them. He needs a real example. He selects her because she is bent and crippled. Could it be when he sees her he is reminded of how the Jewish people are crushed under the weight of both Mosaic Law and Roman law?

Reading further in verses 14-17, we learn the synagogue ruler became indignant and chastised people for trying to be healed on the Sabbath day. Jesus reacts with righteous anger. He not only rebukes this synagogue ruler but also scolds all those around him. He says:

> "'You hypocrites! Doesn't each of you on the Sabbath untie his ox or donkey from the stall and lead it out to give it water? Then should not this woman, a daughter of Abraham whom Satan has kept bound for eighteen long years, be set free on the Sabbath day from what has bound her?' 'When he said this, all his opponents were humiliated, but the people were delighted with all the wonderful things he was doing.'"

Notice Jesus calls her a "daughter of Abraham." He wants people to know she is under the covenant God made with Abraham.

> "When Abram was ninety-nine years old, the Lord appeared to him and said, 'I am God Almighty; walk before me faithfully and be blameless. Then I will make my covenant between me and you and will greatly increase your numbers.'" — Genesis 17:1-2

The Abrahamic covenant is not the Law of Moses. It is an unconditional covenant. This covenant is between God and Abraham, but Abraham is not required to do anything but "walk before me faithfully." God does everything. Abraham is under the grace of God. He is not required to follow any law but to be faithful to God.

The Law of Moses was placed on the people of Israel because they rejected his original covenant with Abraham. They wanted the sort of laws they could follow to prove they were righteous. Unfortunately, the Old Testament is full of sad, tragic examples of how the Jews fell short of keeping the Law.

After this great miracle, when everyone is delighted, Jesus still has more to say. He is not about to let the significance of the crippled woman's healing go without further teaching. Right afterward (Luke 13:18-21), he relates two important parables about the kingdom of God.

> "Then Jesus asked, 'What is the kingdom of God like? What shall I compare it to? It is like a mustard seed, which a man took and planted in his garden. It grew and became a tree, and the birds perched in its branches.' Again he asked, 'What shall I compare the kingdom of God to? It is like yeast that a woman took and mixed into about sixty pounds of flour until it worked all through the dough.'"

In Matthew 13:10, the disciples ask Jesus, "Why do you teach in parables?" We may wonder the same thing. *The Message* gives a good explanation of why Jesus teaches in parables. [Note: *The Message* is a newer, popular translation of the Bible. It is not to be considered as a study Bible, but as a "reading Bible." The Greek words have been translated into English words we use today.] In some instances, such as this, it adds a new perspective:

> "You've been given insight into God's kingdom. You

know how it works. Not everybody has this gift, this insight; it hasn't been given to them. Whenever someone has a ready heart for this, the insights and understandings flow freely. But if there is no readiness, any trace of receptivity soon disappears. That's why I tell stories: to create readiness, to nudge the people toward receptive insight. In their present state they can stare till doomsday and not see it, listen till they're blue in the face and not get it." — Matthew 13:11-15 (*The Message*)

In Psalms 78:2, in prophecy David states: "I will open my mouth in parables, I will utter hidden things, things from of old."

What are we to make of these two parables imparted right after the crippled woman's healing? When Jesus asks, "What is the kingdom of God like?" we look eagerly for the answer. However, he hides it in parables. The Holy Spirit will impart its meaning to those who have "a ready heart."

The parable of the mustard seed is well known, so I want to concentrate on the parable with the woman cook as the star player. The kingdom of "God is like yeast… " What happens when active yeast is worked into the dough? It rises. The dough doubles in size: Yeast is an agent of transformation. This parable has always been troubling to me because Jesus also warns his disciples to be careful of the "yeast of the Pharisees and Sadducees" (Matthew 16:6).

In most Old Testament scriptures, yeast represents sin or pride. A tiny kernel of sin can grow into a greater sin. Those with a lot of "yeast," such as the Pharisees, are puffed up and bloated with sin and pride. However, in this parable, Jesus compares it to the Kingdom of God. The yeast in this instance is likened to the Holy Spirit, acting as a transformative agent on lifeless souls (flour).

Jesus pictures a woman as the person who works the dough. He could have said, "the kingdom of God is like yeast and when it is worked through 60 pounds of flour... " But he does not use a neutral analogy. He references a woman.

Through this, he validates women as useful to the Holy Spirit. They "work the dough" and expand God's kingdom. We don't want to take this analogy too far, but, as women, we see far too few examples of how women play a role in the Kingdom of God and it is refreshing to have Jesus bring us forward, from the back to the front; from obscurity and ostracism to prominence and acceptance as important participants in God's plan.

~ ~ ~ ~ ~

MEDITATION

Sometimes our lives can be bone crushing due to excessive worry. We succumb to stress over details until we can think of nothing else. Worry is not in our true nature. It is a sin.

If you are worried, give your concerns to Jesus, who said, "Take my yoke upon you, and learn from me, for I am gentle and humble in heart, and you will find rest for your souls" (Matthew 11:29). What does Jesus mean to "learn" from him? Meditate on this scripture until it sinks deep into your heart and you know you believe it.

Look at the birds of the air; they do not sow or reap or store away in barns, and yet your heavenly Father feeds them. Are you not much more valuable than they? Can any one of you by worrying add a single hour to your life? — Matthew 6:26-27

Study Guide Questions

CRIPPLED WOMAN

— List three things you want to remember about the Crippled Woman.

— Why did Jesus call the crippled woman up to the front? What does this say about how Jesus views women?

— What is the significance of this healing occurring in a synagogue in front of a group of religious leaders?

— Do you ever feel completely bent over with sin, bitterness, or sorrow? How can you apply this story to your own life? Read Matthew 11:28-30. How does Jesus feel about your burden? What does he ask you to do? Explain.

— Why did Jesus feature a woman in his parable to explain the Kingdom of God? What does the parable mean?

— Are you willing to step forward as the crippled woman, ignoring the possible stares and disapproval of men, and answer Jesus' call? What kind of pushback might you get and how can you respond to it?

NOTES

VIII

WIDOW OF NAIN

Luke's Gospel recounts this resurrection story, which is often over-looked because it is so short and lacking in fanfare. However, it provides us with an important example of Jesus' particular compassion for women in a patriarchal society. In this encounter with a grieving mother who has not only lost her son but also her own livelihood, Jesus is greatly moved by her plight. He understands what she faces. He stops and goes to great lengths to restore what was lost and to give her an abundant life.

This moving story is found in Luke 7:11-16:

> "Soon afterward, Jesus went to a town called Nain, and his disciples and a large crowd went along with him. As he approached the town gate, a dead person was being carried out — the only son of his mother, a widow. And a large crowd from the town was with her.

> "When the Lord saw her, his heart went out to her and he

said, 'Don't cry.' Then he went up and touched the coffin, and those carrying it stood still. He said, 'Young man, I say to you, get up!' The dead man sat up and began to talk, and Jesus gave him back to his mother.

"They were all filled with awe and praised God. 'A great prophet has appeared among us,' they said. 'God has come to help his people.'"

I became a follower of Jesus when I encountered his great love for the first time. Prompted by his Holy Spirit, I faced my sinful and rebellious life and was convicted by my guilt. I repented and instantaneously the Lord filled me with his Holy Spirit and I experienced his miraculous grace, peace and love. I was fully restored and vowed to follow Jesus for the rest of my days.

A few years later when I was a young wife and mother, I had the responsibility of running the home while my husband worked. I spent my free time reading Christian books and studying the Bible, praying and interceding for others. My husband was in the military and worked long hours, which meant he did not have the same opportunity to study the Bible as I did.

During our weekly Bible study and at Sunday school, I shared what I had learned and thought my contributions were appreciated. My husband often had to go away on temporary duty assignments and I was left to handle things alone. Out of necessity, I took care of the children by myself and became quite self-reliant.

One Sunday, the whole family went to church together. Our Sunday school teacher announced he was leaving and would need to find a replacement. I went to the pastor and told him I was interested in teaching. He informed me because it was a mixed group it was unscriptural for me to teach because I was a woman. I was shocked.

This was the first time I encountered First Timothy 2:12 ("I do not permit a woman to teach or to assume authority over a man; she must be quiet."). I was devastated and my spirit was squashed.

It took many years of intense study before I was able to understand and reconcile the incongruity of this scripture. The epistle of First Timothy is Paul's letter to Timothy, a young, inexperienced pastor, instructing him on how to handle specific issues. One of those issues was a flood of converted Gentile women unschooled in Jewish beliefs who were taking over the church and causing confusion.

Although this was Paul's answer to a specific issue, this scripture has frequently been used as a holy hammer to keep women in their place, completely ignoring Paul's overall teaching on freedom in Christ.

> "It is for freedom that Christ has set us free. Stand firm, then, and do not let yourselves be burdened again with the yoke of slavery." — Galatians 5:1

When my husband was named the new Sunday school teacher I was surprised because they knew he often had to go out of town. Sure enough, it wasn't long before he was called away. The church canceled Sunday school rather than have me fill in for him.

That night, after a particularly trying day of taking care of the children, fixing a clogged toilet, filling the car's tires with air, and nailing down a step on the back porch, I went to my knees, crying to the Lord. "Why God? Why did you make me a woman? Why did you give me this brain if I can't use it? Why give me spiritual knowledge if I'm not allowed to teach what I've learned?"

I will never forget that moment. My heart was filled with an agony of frustration. I couldn't believe God was so unfair. I couldn't believe God had made me so inferior and untrustworthy that I couldn't even teach Sunday school. If Adam was his first human, surely Eve must be perceived as the new and improved version. How could my gender disqualify me from fulfilling my purpose? How could my knowledge be of no value to the men in the church?

"Why God? Why make me a woman?"

He answered me through his Word.

> "But who are you, a human being, to talk back to God? Shall what is formed say to the one who formed it, 'Why did you make me like this?'" Does not the potter have the right to make out of the same lump of clay some pottery for special purposes and some for common use?"
> — Romans 9:20-21

For years, I was deeply hurt by what I had perceived to be his answer. I immediately assumed God was saying I was for common use — an ordinary housewife with nothing to contribute but cooking, cleaning and raising children (which I then accepted as my life's purpose).

It wasn't until I meditated on the story of the Widow of Nain that I became aware of God's heart for women. I was not common. Jesus had called me for a special purpose — to be all he created me to be.

I learned he is not ignorant of what women face. He understands our plight in a patriarchal society. He knows what it's like to be silenced. He doesn't burden us with a yoke of slavery. He offers us abundant life.

My situation may appear unfair, but how much harder and unjust was life for the Widow of Nain? During her time, the death of a child is certainly devastating, but when a child's loss carries the mother's own *de facto* death sentence along with it, the widow's grief is beyond our comprehension.

Previous to the story of the Widow of Nain as written in the Gospel of Luke, Jesus has come from Capernaum where Jewish elders have approached him on behalf of a Roman centurion, a godly man who helped build their synagogue. As Jesus nears the centurion's house, the man's servants intercept him to say their master doesn't need Jesus to make an appearance but to only speak the word and his servant would be healed.

Jesus marvels over this faith because a Gentile has greater faith and understanding of the Kingdom of God than his own Jewish brethren. With a word, Jesus heals the servant without ever seeing him, without being in his presence. He somewhat rebukes his disciples when he points out how faith works, even when it comes from a Gentile. From there, Jesus travels to Nain, a trip of some thirty miles, crossing the Sea of Galilee.

As usual, wherever Jesus goes a crowd follows him. This includes the twelve Apostles, his disciples, both male and female, Jews, Gentiles, seekers of truth, and the curious, hoping to see Jesus perform another miracle. This large group is with him as he approaches the town of Nain, which is situated at the base of Mount Tabor in Galilee, about ten miles southeast of Nazareth. As they come to the city gates, prepared to pass through, an equally large crowd is coming out and confronts them.

Those accompanying Jesus at the time have seen the lame walk, the blind see, the deaf hear, demons cast out, water turned to wine and storms stilled by his word. Even with the constant criticism of other religious leaders, his followers are excited and jubilant. They are experiencing a time of wonder and miracles; their Messiah has come, and they get to be with him. People are drawn to Jesus. He emanates goodness, peace, joy and love. All the fruits of the Spirit manifest through him. He is without sin. He is unlike any other man.

Even though we know he got angry, felt heartbreak, and suffered sorrow for the lost; for the most part during his active ministry he is truly the Light of the World and being in his physical presence is a time of overwhelming joy and happiness.

I imagine the crowd following him is boisterous, apt to break into song at a moment's notice, full of laughter and animated conversation. This is what it is like to be in Jesus' presence. It is not an occasion for somber reflection on the weight of your sin. It is joyous and liberating. It is filled with the glory of God's everlasting love.

As this great crowd of happy people comes to the gates of Nain they confront the opposite. The group leaving Nain is not laughing, singing or talking. They are wailing and crying with grief, covered in ashes of mourning. A spirit of death hangs over them. At the gates of Nain, great joy meets great sorrow. Light meets darkness. Life meets death.

Jesus and his followers step aside to allow these mourners to exit the town. The laughter and singing have stopped. They bow their heads and honor the funeral procession. At the head of the crowd, men carry a coffin with the corpse of a young man who has died before his time.

Next to the coffin is the young man's mother, weeping uncontrollably. She can barely walk. Her legs are like rubber and her heart is so heavy she can barely breathe. She is probably supported on either side by relatives, friends, neighbors or paid mourners because we can imagine she can barely see through her tears and the crushing weight of her grief.

The scriptures state this is a large funeral procession. We can surmise the young man's mother is a person of some wealth and prestige and we quickly learn she is also widowed, compounding her grief. The young man in the coffin is her only son; the heir of her fortunes, the bearer of her husband's name and her future hopes.

As a widow without an heir, she cannot inherit the land. She is now completely alone and will become dependent on relatives or the charity of others. With his death, everything she had hoped for is gone. Without an heir, her husband's family line will end. Her purpose for living died with him.

There is no greater grief for a mother than to bury her child. Since her husband has preceded her in death, she has no one close to her to help her bear the burden of grief, and to compound that, she has now lost her position in society. Without her son, she is nobody. "When the Lord saw her, his heart went out to her and he said, 'don't cry'" (v.13).

It is important to note Jesus is not looking at the dead man. He is looking at the young man's mother. He knows this is a funeral procession, but his eyes seek out the one left behind, the widow with the broken heart. His eyes quickly find her. At that moment, this woman, this grieving mother, is all he sees. And the scriptures state, "When he saw her his heart went out to her." His heart did not go out to the dead man who has died before his time, but to the man's mother.

His heart went out to her. No matter what translation you read, Jesus is greatly moved by this woman's plight. Some say, "he had compassion on her," others say "when he saw her, his heart broke." Whichever translation you read, it is a poignant moment when Jesus looks at this woman and nearly weeps for her.

His only thought is to restore what is taken from her. He has power over death. If he chooses, he can raise this woman's son and return him to her whole and healthy. It is important we see Jesus is motivated by the woman's heartbreak, not by the untimely demise of her son. This is our Lord.

Through this encounter, Jesus demonstrates how much he loves women, and reveals his compassion for their lot in life. Is anything more pitiful than this woman's fate? She is at the mercy of a patriarchal society, which makes her penniless and destitute because her only son has died and she is a widow. Not only has she suffered the loss of her husband, but also the loss of her only son and is now at the mercy of others to sustain her life. Jesus is well aware of the injustice of society toward women. He cannot let her pass without speaking to her. He says, "Don't cry."

Although it might seem a stretch, I think that in witnessing this funeral procession and the mother's grief, Jesus confronts his own impending death and the grief it will cause his mother. Does he picture his mother's face distorted in grief? When he looks on the young man's face, does he see his own fate? Does he see the crowd of his followers, one moment laughing and joking, then suddenly bowed with solemnity at the finality of death?

I can't imagine what went through his mind when confronted with this tableau of the death of a beloved son, but whatever he is thinking passes quickly through his mind and he steps forward and speaks only to the widow of Nain, making everyone stop.

"Don't cry," he tells her.

Does he touch her? Does he put his hand on her shoulder? Does he wipe away her tears? Does he shout to be heard above the mourners? Does he bend down and whisper in her ear? We do not know. All we know is he speaks only to her and the funeral procession stops.

"Don't cry." His words must stun her and those who hear him. Was he being insensitive? She is wrapped in incredible grief. Of course, she is crying; crying with a broken heart. Who is this man who tells her to stop crying? However, as I noted before, Jesus carries the fullness of the Spirit of God's great love for humanity. He is filled with compassion for her. His words evoke love and peace. I think she knows this instantly, as soon as he speaks.

The scriptures state he then went up to the coffin and touched it, making the entire funeral procession stop. Why does it stop? Was his presence so full of light and authority that when he approaches them everything stops? It is not recorded that anyone confronts him. We can certainly imagine Jesus has a certain quality that brings power, authority and love to the situation

According to the scriptures, it happens quickly. There is no time for people to say, "This is Jesus, the great Healer." "This is the Messiah." "This is the Son of God." His presence alone commands their obedience.

"He said, 'Young man, I say to you, get up!' The dead man sits up and begins to talk..." Imagine this. The corpse of a young man suddenly rises up and begins to talk. How did it happen? Jesus commanded the corpse to get up.

The brevity of his words is stunning. He does not open his arms wide, appeal to Jehovah and pray a long involved prayer. He does not go away, fast and prepare himself for the greatest fight of his life — the resurrection of the dead. He addresses the man and commands him to "get up" and he rises. It is similar to when he commanded the waves on the Sea of Galilee to "be still!" and the sea was calm. He commands a dead man to "get up!" and the corpse comes to life.

It is worth noting that the spirit of this dead young man hears Jesus and returns to his body. Where is the young man's spirit? Obviously, he is in the spirit realm. He hears and obeys Jesus' command.

It is a wonder the men carrying the coffin didn't drop it right then and there, shout in fear and run away — probably because it happens instantaneously, their minds cannot comprehend it.

The scriptures state the young man sits up and begins to talk. What does he say? "What's going on?" or "Mother, why are you crying?" or "I have seen the glory of God!" or "I was dead but now am alive!" We do not know what he says, but we know he is talking, indicating his mind is restored to him. The young man is in possession of his faculties.

The scriptures then say, "and Jesus gave him back to his mother" (v. 15). How precious is that? This is further indication Jesus has been entirely motivated from beginning to end by restoration of this mother's broken heart and broken life. What death stole from her, Jesus restores. We can imagine once they realize the corpse is no longer a corpse, the men set the coffin on the ground and Jesus helps the young man to his feet and leads him to his mother, who embraces him with fear, trembling and great joy.

Can you imagine what she is thinking? All hope was gone, and now hope returns. Her dead son is now alive. Her encounter with Jesus goes beyond her ability to have faith. In so many of his personal meetings with women, Jesus says, "your faith has healed you." However, the widow of Nain has no faith to believe her son will come back from the dead. She is the recipient of God's love and grace. She did not do anything to deserve the greatest of all Jesus' miracles. It is only due to his compassion and his love for her. When he sees her, his heart breaks for her. This is the God we serve.

Remember there are two great crowds surrounding this scene — those who are following the Light of the World and those who are following Death. Both groups are astounded by what has happened. If any of those in either crowd have any doubt Jesus is the Messiah, their own eyes must now convince them. The scriptures go on to say those who witnessed this event "were filled with awe and praised God." They begin to declare Jesus is a great prophet and say "God has come to help his people" (v. 16).

They have witnessed the resurrection of the dead and call Jesus a great prophet. They are most likely comparing him to the prophet Elisha who raised the Shunammite woman's son from death because the town of Nain is only a couple miles from Shunem where this Old Testament miracle was to have taken place (see 2 Kings 4:8-36).

In this instance, Jesus speaks but a few words. He says, "Young man, I say to you, get up!" In front of a huge crowd, the man in the coffin sits up and begins to talk. What does Jesus do next? He gives him "back to his mother" (v. 15). In a split second, the Widow of Nain's fortune, position, and broken heart are completely restored by a loving and compassionate Savior. He gives her an abundant life.

~ ~ ~ ~ ~

MEDITATION

Grief comes in many ways — the loss of a job, the loss of a marriage, the death of a dream, the passing of a loved one. There is only One who can restore your peace in the midst of great tragedy or loss. Jesus is the One who heals the broken-hearted. He can ease your pain.

Close your eyes. Imagine a box at your feet. Put your grief, your loss, your pain inside, and then imagine placing this box in Jesus' hands. Leave it there and accept his healing and his love.

The Lord is near the broken-hearted; he is the Savior of those whose spirits are crushed down. — *Psalms 34:18*

Study Guide Questions

WIDOW OF NAIN

— List three things you want to remember about the Widow of Nain.

— Why does this woman move Jesus so deeply? What does it say about him? What does it say about how he relates to women?

— Do you feel like you are made for common use and not for a special purpose? Discuss how being a child of God makes you special and being called by the Most High God gives you a special purpose in life.

— This is the second resurrection recorded in the Gospels. Discuss how Jesus raised the son from the dead. How does it compare to other resurrections? (Read Luke 8:51-55 and John 11:33-44) Do you believe in the resurrection of the dead? Discuss what this means.

— Have you ever experienced a loss? Do you believe God wants to restore to you what was lost? Why or why not? Discuss different ways in which God might restore your loss. How does the story of the Widow of Nain give you faith for restoration?

— Do you know a widow? Is there an organized support system for the widowed in your church or study group? If not, what steps can you take to help meet that need?

NOTES

IX

GENEROUS WOMAN

This story of the generous woman, who was also a widow, is not a personal encounter but an endearing portrait of how Jesus views women. This account is found in the Gospels of Mark and Luke. The following is from Luke 21:1-4.

> "As Jesus looked up, he saw the rich putting their gifts into the temple treasury. He also saw a poor widow put in two very small copper coins. 'Truly I tell you,' he said, 'this poor widow has put in more than all the others. All these people gave their gifts out of their wealth; but she out of her poverty put in all she had to live on.'"

The Gospel of Mark's story differs only in the context of setting — Jesus sits across from the temple treasury watching as people put in their offerings. It is a relaxed atmosphere, but Jesus is intently watching. The way offerings and sacrifices are made is of great concern to him.

One cannot help but consider the last prophet of the Old Testament,

Malachi, who foretold of these events in chapter 3:1-4:

> "I will send my messenger, who will prepare the way before me. Then suddenly the Lord you are seeking will come to his temple; the messenger of the covenant, whom you desire, will come,' says the Lord Almighty.

> "But who can endure the day of his coming? Who can stand when he appears? For he will be a refiner and purifier of silver; he will purify the Levites and refine them like gold and silver.

> "Then the Lord will have men who will bring offerings in righteousness, and the offerings of Judah and Jerusalem will be acceptable to the Lord, as in days gone by, as in former years."

Let us put this in context to see how Jesus came to make his observation about the woman's offering. Only a few days earlier, Jesus enters Jerusalem riding on a donkey. The people laid cloaks on the path and waved palm fronds, shouting "Blessed is he who comes in the name of the Lord!" He immediately goes to the temple, looks around, seeing both the commerce and the larceny and leaves for Bethany, probably to Martha's house since he is always welcome.

The next day Jesus goes back to the temple and "He overturned the table of the money changers and the benches of those selling doves, and would not allow anyone to carry merchandise through the temple courts" (Mark 11:15-16). When the temple priests hear of this they want to kill him, but he is so popular they choose to bide their time. Jesus and his disciples leave the city.

When they return to the temple the next day, not surprisingly, the Pharisees confront him and demand to know by whose authority he does what he does: healing, preaching, and overturning money tables. Jesus refuses to respond. It appears that he is still upset and figures it isn't worth his time to explain his actions.

They send others to catch up to him and he responds to them in parables — primarily about money, taxes, and marriage. The crowd loves what he says.

He warns them to beware of the teachers of the Law: "They devour widows' houses and for a show make lengthy prayers. These men will be punished most severely" (Luke 20:47). It appears that in Jesus' eyes, defrauding widows is the worst kind of crime, next to hypocrisy.

With all this in mind, Jesus sits across from the treasury, watching people deposit their offerings. Along comes a lone woman. Through his close observation, he can see she is a poor widow, probably because she is wearing worn and tattered garments of mourning.

We know from other examples Jesus has a soft spot in his heart for widows. It is probably why he is watching her so closely. Perhaps a rich man comes before her and makes a big deal about how much he is putting in the treasury. Jesus has spent several days observing the larceny, hypocrisy and injustice going on in God's holy temple. He is feeling quite sad about the state of the people of Israel.

Then along comes this widow. We do not know how old she is or why she is alone, but we can guess she is not young, but an older woman who has no resources, no sons to accompany her, and only two small coins to give the Kingdom of God.

How does Jesus see how much she is putting into the treasury box? How does he know it is all she has? He may have observed it; then again, Jesus operates in the supernatural. He has foresight and the gift of knowledge. He can see her heart, know her financial deprivation and observe she gives all she has.

In "seeing" this, his heart is lightened. He is touched by her generosity and her faith. It is one thing to give your tithes to the Lord, but it is another thing altogether to give all you have to the Lord. This is powerful faith.

I have a close friend who is a widow. Her husband died after a long illness, leaving her with three daughters, hospital bills, and an uncertain future. While she was in the depth of her grief she had to muster up courage, fortitude and energy to keep the wolves at bay. She lost her main source of income. She lost her house. She lost her loving companion. She lost her plans for the future. In the midst of this devastating loss, she had to forge a new life. However, she is not to be pitied. She is a woman of faith and I have seen how she draws upon the Spirit of God to give her the strength she needs to go on. She struggles. It is not an easy road and she would never turn away a helping hand.

When I see her I remember how the Lord's heart is constantly moved by the plight of widows, how much he admires them, how his heart goes out to them. Here is an area of ministry overlooked today.

My hope is that the church will rise to the occasion and provide support and succor to Christian widows. I encourage all Christian women to make sure there is a support system to help widows and thus gladden our Lord's heart.

Our Gospel writer, Luke, is either not able to find this widow woman or did not deem the rest of her story important to the account. Of course, I want to know what happened to her.

Knowing as we do Christ brought the new Covenant of grace into the world, I wonder how this woman who touched the Lord's heart with gladness and compassion fared after she gave "everything she owned" as her token of faith in God. I believe through her seed of faith a great harvest grew. I do not know this for a fact, but I believe it one hundred percent.

This is how the Kingdom of God operates. Total surrender brings great harvest. It is a spiritual principle.

~ ~ ~ ~ ~

MEDITATION

Although tithing is not a New Testament precept, giving ten percent of your assets to the Lord brings remarkable blessings. This does not only mean money. It can be your time, your voice, or your service. Wherever you receive your spiritual nourishment, give from your heart and be generous.

Each of you should give what you have decided in your heart to give, not reluctantly or under compulsion, for God loves a cheerful giver. — 2 Corinthians 9:7

Study Guide Questions

GENEROUS WOMAN

— List three things you want to remember about the Generous Woman.

— Why does this woman's action move Jesus so much?

— Does "giving all" mean materially or figuratively or both? What does sacrificial giving mean to you?

— How does Jesus know how much money the woman gave? What did Jesus mean when he said she "gave out of her poverty"? Why is this important?

— Does Jesus take issue with the way the rich give their money? Why? How should the rich give? What is the lesson here for those who are prosperous?

— Does tithing affect your personal prosperity? Do you have an example of how sowing seeds in faith caused an increase in your life?

NOTES

X

CANAANITE WOMAN

Jesus' encounter with the Canaanite Woman is one of the most complicated stories we have about our Lord and his relationship with women. For years, I skipped over this story because I could not understand this personal encounter. Matthew 15:21-28 outlines the whole story:

"Leaving that place, Jesus withdrew to the region of Tyre and Sidon. A Canaanite woman from that vicinity came to him, crying out, 'Lord, Son of David, have mercy on me! My daughter is demon-possessed and suffering terribly.' Jesus did not answer a word. So his disciples came to him and urged him, 'Send her away, for she keeps crying out after us.' He answered, 'I was sent only to the lost sheep of Israel.'

The woman came and knelt before him. 'Lord, help me!' she said. He replied, 'It is not right to take the children's bread and toss it to the dogs.' 'Yes it is, Lord,' she said.

'Even the dogs eat the crumbs that fall from their master's table.' Then Jesus said to her, 'Woman, you have great faith! Your request is granted.' And her daughter was healed at that moment."

When I read about Jesus' encounter with the Canaanite woman in Matthew 15:21-28, or the "Greek Syrophoenician" woman as she is identified in Mark 7:24-30; what strikes me the most is Jesus' seemingly rather insulting and dismissive response to this woman. It is uncharacteristic. Why is he mean to her? Why does he appear to be no different from all the other men who have dismissed and insulted women throughout the ages? What is happening here? Is he validating chauvinism? Is he confirming our worst fears that women are of little value and a nuisance to men?

This is why this particular encounter is so important for us as women to examine and understand. If your heart is telling you there has to be more here than what meets the eye, then you are right. This encounter is set apart from all others. To understand it better, we need to put it in perspective by looking at what has previously occurred.

In Matthew 14, we learn John the Baptist, a powerful prophet and Jesus' beloved cousin, has been beheaded (vv. 1-12). This must have been a shock to Jesus and his disciples — many were baptized by John, even Jesus. We know Jesus is affected because the scripture says when he hears of it, he "withdrew by boat privately to a solitary place" (v. 13).

However, the crowds follow. Jesus responds. "He had compassion on them and healed their sick" (v. 14). When evening falls, the disciples want to send the people away, but Jesus instead feeds the large crowd with five loaves of bread and two fish. Once they have eaten and are satisfied "the disciples picked up twelve basketfuls of broken pieces that were leftover. The number of those who ate was about five thousand men, besides women and children" (vv. 15-21).

Here is an example of God's compassion for his people (including women and children) and His provision is beyond what is expected. He not only feeds them but feeds them until they are full — and with leftovers for later. Keep this in mind when we get to the Canaanite woman.

Jesus sends his disciples out ahead on a boat. He spends a little more time with the crowd before he dismisses them and goes to the mountain to pray by himself. I suspect he needs some time alone to grieve for his cousin John and to pray about the fate he knows will be his own.

It is late evening before Jesus comes down from the mountain. By that time, the disciples are a "considerable distance from shore." Jesus appears to them, walking on the water and it scares them to death. We all know this story (Matthew 14:22-31). Peter wants to do it, too. He takes a few steps, sees the waves, and begins to sink. Jesus catches him and says, "You of little faith, why did you doubt?" When they get to shore, there is another crowd waiting for him. The scripture states they beg him to let their sick touch his cloak, "and all who touched it were healed" (v. 36). All who touched it were healed. No one was excluded.

At the beginning of Matthew 15, Jesus is confronted by a group of angry Pharisees who have come down from Jerusalem to confront him and blast him because his disciples are not washing their hands before they eat, according to the law. Jesus has a heated exchange with these religious leaders and calls them "hypocrites." He quotes from Isaiah 29:13: "These people come near to me with their mouth and honor me with their lips, but their hearts are far from me. Their worship of me is based on merely human rules they have been taught." Remember this passage when we come to the Canaanite woman.

In Matthew 15:10, Jesus explains what goes into the mouth does not defile you; it is what comes out of it that defiles you. The disciples do not understand. Jesus becomes exasperated: "Are you so dull? Don't you see that whatever enters the mouth goes into the stomach and then out of the body? But the things that come out of a person's mouth come from the heart, and these defile them." He is trying to explain to them the difference between clean and unclean, between holiness and pretense, between lips of worship and hearts of worship, but they are not getting it. In fact, they are worried Jesus may have offended the Pharisees.

Later, in Matthew 23:27, Jesus makes it clear in no uncertain terms what he thinks of hypocrisy: "Woe to you, teachers of the law and Pharisees, you hypocrites! You are like whitewashed tombs, which look beautiful on the outside, but on the inside are full of the bones of the dead and everything unclean." Jesus has harsh words for those who enforce laws based on physical appearances while neglecting the spirit or the heart within. It is not how you appear on the outside; it is what is in your heart.

Enter the Canaanite woman.

In these previous scriptures, Jesus is experiencing all the weaknesses of being human. He is grieving over John's death, exasperated with his disciples for their dull-wittedness, and furious with the Jewish leaders who focus on the minutia of their law while their people are begging to be fed and healed.

This is who Jesus is. It says in Hebrews 4:15: "For we do not have a high priest who is not able to sympathize with our weaknesses, but we have one who has been tempted in every way, just as we are — yet was without sin."

When we think about Jesus in the flesh, we must not deify him to the exclusion of his humanity. He walked, he ate, he slept, he cried, he loved, he laughed and he got exasperated and angry; and yet was without sin. Through the encounter with the Canaanite woman, we glimpse Jesus' humanity, and it is a woman who reminds him of heavenly truths.

Who is this woman? Mark calls her a Syrophoenician (of Syria-Phoenicia) and Matthew calls her a Canaanite? Mark's account is the more accurate description since she comes from that region; however, Matthew is trying to make a point about her. At the time of Matthew's writing, they are not known as Canaanites, but Syrophoenicians.

The Canaanites were an ancient people (Canaan was the grandson of Noah) who were a constant menace to the Israelites throughout the Old Testament. We all know about the Canaanites from Exodus when Moses leads the Israelites into the land of Canaan. The region this woman hails from is also where the ancient and wicked Queen Jezebel lived and sought the life of Elijah. It was a land of paganism and blatant prejudice. Naming this woman a "Canaanite" is Matthew's way of saying "you know, those hated pagans who have plagued us since the beginning, the ones who have robbed and killed us!" There is no love lost between the Syrophoenicians and the Jews.

She may be a wealthy woman. She is living in a prosperous area, an urban city, and in Mark's account, he identifies her as a Greek; which is to say she comes from the upper classes since Hellenization occurred in the educated community first. This also gives credence to the notion she is "in-the-know" about this Jewish rabbi who is creating quite a stir down south with stories of miraculous healing at his touch. If she is a woman of means, then it signifies she has already tried every treatment available to heal her daughter.

Her screaming and debasement to a Jew — odd behavior for a woman of means — show us how desperate she is. In addition, in verse 30, Mark states, "And when she was come to her house, she found the devil gone out, and her daughter laid upon her bed" (KJV). So we know she has a house — which doesn't necessarily mean she has money — but Mark also states her daughter is "upon her bed," using the word *klinē*, meaning couch or furniture.[12] This is indicative of a well-to-do household.

Of course, she is a woman. In my opinion, the Grecian view of women is probably the worst — and we experience its effects even into the 21st century. The great Greek philosopher, Aristotle, believed women were inferior to men in a number of ways — physically, emotionally, and intellectually. Besides being inferior, they had no role in society except to take care of their husbands, keep the household running smoothly for his pleasure, and bear his children. According to Aristotle's view, women were only slightly higher than slaves on the social scale. It was his contention men were "apt to lead" but women were not because their souls lacked authority.[13]

We will leave for another time the comparison of Hellenization and its impact on the Christian church's view of women. Still, our "Canaanite" woman is able to travel freely on the streets and is unaccompanied by a man. Either she is flouting the law in her desperation or there are no restrictions placed on women in the area.

Prior to meeting this Canaanite woman, Jesus leaves Gennesaret on the northwest shore of the Sea of Galilee and goes to "the region of Tyre and Sidon." This is a considerable distance north, about 30 to 40 miles from where they are. Tyre and Sidon are prosperous seaports and across the border from the northern tip of Galilee. They are ancient Phoenician cities with a long history of paganism. According to Mark, Jesus did not actually go into Tyre but to the border; but Matthew indicates he entered the area, crossing the border between the land of Galilee and the land of Syria Phoenicia.

It is curious that Jesus goes north at this time, especially all the way into Syria Phoenicia, the land of Gentiles. Thirty or forty miles by foot will have taken at least a day. We can only guess at his state of mind. He is tired, exasperated and sorrowful and has recently had a profound mountaintop experience with God. We don't know what transpired between Father and Son, but when he next comes face-to-face with the Canaanite woman there occurs a significant change in his ministry.

The scripture says in Matthew 15:21: "Leaving that place, Jesus withdrew to the region of Tyre and Sidon." He withdrew. The Greek word for this is *anachōreō*, meaning to depart or seek another place out of fear.[14] *Webster's Dictionary* gives another meaning of "withdraw" as being "to draw back from a battlefield."[15] This appears more appropriate. I do not think Jesus is running away out of fear, but I do think he has been through a battle. He needs to recuperate, to get as far away from the crowds and the Pharisees as he possibly can. He goes where he will not be known.

Immediately upon arriving, a Canaanite woman cries out, "Lord, Son of David, have mercy on me! My daughter is demon-possessed and suffering terribly." She cries out. This woman has learned Jesus, the Healer, is in town and she is desperate for him to heal her daughter. She is in an agony of despair. She has only one hope — the Savior of the Jews will heal her daughter. Her plaintive cry must have touched his heart; but what does Jesus say?

Nothing. Matthew 15:23 states, "Jesus did not answer a word."

Does this surprise us? We know from previous scriptures Jesus heals all who come to him and turns none away; but here he appears to be ignoring her. Many commentaries try to explain Jesus' lack of response, but the one I like the best is a brief note from John Wesley, an eighteenth century theologian and founder of the Methodist Church. He said, "He [Jesus] sometimes tries our faith in like manner."[16]

Perhaps, because of what she is saying, how she is addressing him, he knows her heart and chooses to test her faith — give her an opportunity to exercise her faith through persistence. On the other hand, perhaps he hopes if he ignores her she will go away and leave him alone.

She is persistent and will not go away. His lack of response does not deter her. As they continue walking, she continues to cry out, shouting, screaming for Jesus to heal her daughter — so much so that the disciples urge him to "Send her away, for she keeps crying out after us." (Notice how the disciples are always trying to send people away.)

Here is Jesus walking, minding his own business, trying to get some peace and quiet away from the crowds, and this fanatical woman is screaming and running after them, "Lord, Son of David, have mercy on me!" You can imagine the disciples' reaction; turning and giving her foul looks or waving their arms at her to go away as they hurry after Jesus who keeps walking. The farther they walk away, the more her voice becomes shrill.

"Lord, Son of David, have mercy on me!"

The first thing we notice, besides her screaming, is she is calling Jesus "Lord, Son of David." This is significant because this Canaanite has to be aware of what it means to call someone "Lord, Son of David." She is calling out the Messianic title. She is acknowledging Jesus is the Messiah. How she comes by this knowledge we do not know. She has probably heard about the numerous miracles he has performed and has concluded he must be the Jews' Messiah. Or she is given holy insight.

How does Jesus respond to this unexpected declaration of praise and acknowledgement by this desperate foreign woman? He answers, "I was sent only to the lost sheep of Israel" (v. 24). It is a curious rebuff and quite uncharacteristic of Jesus. Isn't this the same Jesus who says to his disciples after his resurrection in Mark 16:15: "go into all the world and preach the gospel to all creation." Something has changed. From the point he meets the Canaanite woman to his resurrection, his ministry, mission, and the new covenant have expanded.

We can also conjecture Jesus is not even talking to the woman. He is walking, he ignores her cries, the disciples say to him, "send her away," and he responds he is only there for the Jews. To whom is he saying this? He is either talking to his disciples or speaking to himself. We know Jesus is born of compassion, not only for the Jews but also for the whole world. If he is talking to his disciples, it is a curious response to their entreaty to get rid of the woman who is bringing unwanted attention to them — they are in the land of Gentiles, a land of prosperous people who are loyal to Rome. I believe they are actually fearful this woman, with her screaming and calling him "Lord, Son of David," will give them away as Jews.

I think Jesus is talking to himself; speaking it aloud to hear it with his own ears. "I was sent only for the lost sheep of Israel." It is as if he is trying to convince himself his mission is clear-cut, at least it was until this woman's desperate cry penetrates his ears and his heart. Maybe he phrases it as more of a question: "I was sent only for the Jews?"

What is it God spoke to him on the mountaintop? Could it be when he poured his heart out to God about the impossibility of his mission to the Jews — how they had chopped off John's head, how his own followers doubted him, and while his people were hungry for bread their leaders were obsessed with whether they'd washed their hands or not — the Father said, "Yes, they are a stiff-necked people and my chosen ones, but I love all of my creation; I would not see any perish." Jesus knows without a doubt he has come to redeem the lost sheep of Israel — at least up until this time he has concentrated only on them.

It also speaks of Jesus' weariness. Everywhere he goes he is beset by hordes of people. He has compassion for them, heals and feeds them, but they keep coming. He goes into Gentile country for a respite, but he is immediately confronted by this woman from the land of the hated Canaanites and has nothing to give her but his theology. Whatever interior dialogue is in Jesus' mind and whatever his intent is, the matter is settled by this foreign woman.

"The woman came and knelt before him" (v. 25). She impedes his progress. Matthew uses the Greek word *proskyne* here, which is "to bow down" or "worship." She prostrates herself before him to worship him. "Lord, help me!" she cries. She has ended whatever argument he has been having with himself or his disciples about who he is there to save. He stops dead in his tracks. He can't step over her or go around her. He must deal with her. She is a Canaanite humbling herself before a Jewish stranger in public. This must be either great mental distress or ferocious maternal courage.

Now he talks to her directly. "It is not right to take the children's bread and toss it to the dogs." Doesn't this appear harsh? She is prostrate before him, begging for help. It is a terrible insult, this reference to dogs (curs), but a common one Jews used to describe their Canaanite neighbors. There is no love lost between Israel and Canaan — to this day. Today the area includes parts of Syria, Israel and the Palestinian territories. The animosity among these cultures is ancient and deep. Jesus is only remarking as the people of his culture would.

I have thought much about this because it is such a troubling statement. I see this woman in an agony of despair willing to bow down and worship a Jew if he can save her daughter, and Jesus all but calls her a dog. Is this the Jesus you know? It is shocking and disturbing. Scholars great and learned have struggled over this passage; some wanting to "spiritualize" it by saying Jesus is merely testing the woman's faith and others insisting he isn't referring to mongrels so much as puppies.[17]

Jesus is having a debate with himself about the extent of his ministry. His comment is one any of his disciples would utter without thinking about it. Maybe one of his disciples has already said it. Let us say Jesus repeats it, or knows it as a common saying among his people, and has heard it himself. Is this what he has come to do, to reject this woman's heartfelt cry for help?

On the other hand, maybe he is saying it for the woman's benefit, as in, "You know, we Jews don't have much and you Syrophoenicians have all the wealth, and now you want me to help you? You want me to take the little we Jews have and give it to you? Do you know what you're asking of me?" I think he is insulting her — for a reason. Remember he has called the Pharisees and leaders of the Law "hypocrites" and worse, and they want to kill him. Now this foreign enemy of his people is at his feet begging for his help. What will she do if he calls her what everyone else calls her people?

She responds right away; not a heartbeat passes: "Yes it is, Lord," she says. "Even the dogs eat the crumbs that fall from their master's table."

It is no wonder Jesus exclaims, "Woman you have great faith!" He is shown at his most harsh, seemingly rejecting her at every turn, and yet through her persistence, she demonstrates great faith, which removes Jesus' qualms. However, it is not only that she is persistent. She is declaring in no uncertain terms Jesus is the Master. Her words show an amazing insight of God's great love.

Psalms 23 says, "He prepares a table before me in the presence of my enemies. My cup runs over." She knows nothing about how Jesus fed more than 5,000 people with five loaves and two fish, collecting twelve basketfuls of leftovers — abundance beyond belief. This woman, this foreign infidel, prostrates herself, humbles herself before Jesus and declares, "I know you are the Messiah and that from your hand comes so much abundance that even the crumbs that fall from your magnificent table will satisfy my hunger."

This episode is the culmination of everything Jesus has been going through over the past few days. After everything that has happened, he may have even questioned the effectiveness of his ministry. I don't think it counts as a sin if Jesus struggles with the seeming futility of his message to hard-hearted, doubting, incredulous, dull-witted people he has been ministering to for some time — many who want to (and will) kill him. Here, in the most unlikely of places, from the most unlikely of persons — a Gentile woman — Jesus finds the great faith he has been hoping to see.

Even his closest friend and disciple Peter does not understand as this woman does. If there had been a lake nearby, she would have followed him over the water — this is why Jesus responds so enthusiastically and instantly. His heart is bursting with joy. Here is one who hears and believes even without seeing one miracle.

I can imagine him stooping and picking her up, hugging her to himself (the scriptures don't give us any indication of this, but I can imagine even if he didn't, he felt like doing it.) He immediately tells her (v. 28), "'your request is granted.' And her daughter was healed at that moment."

I want you to remember verse 10 in which Jesus says, "Don't you see that whatever enters the mouth goes into the stomach and then out of the body? But the things that come out of a person's mouth come from the heart, and these defile them." This is when he was trying to explain the difference between the appearance of godliness and true godliness.

It is not how well we obey the law and its minutia, but what is in our hearts. God is not interested in our service if it is only meaningless ritual to prove how worthy we are; God looks at our heart and knows whether our service is born of worship and love or not. Our heart is what must be redeemed. From the heart will come true worship and our deeds will be born of devotion.

For everything he has done for them; the crowds, the disciples, the Jews, not one of them has an understanding of true worship — true faith. People are so wrapped up in their laws and worldly thinking they are almost unaware of the interior life — the life of the heart. This is what Jesus has come to redeem, not freedom from Rome's occupation and not freedom from Jewish laws. He has come to bring them freedom from Satan's snare that has imprisoned their hearts, making them so hard-hearted, so dull and so exasperatingly narrow-minded.

And in the dust at his feet is this woman from enemy territory whose heart is open, honest, and free of prejudice and bitterness — willing to give all at Jesus' feet. God longs for this kind of heart. This is the attitude he seeks. He seeks a penitent, honest, openhearted soul willing to lay everything down at Jesus' feet. This is the one who will be saved. It is the clearest picture of Jesus we have seen so far. All his questions, heartache, exasperation and frustration melt away in an instant through the example of this woman's faith. Jesus has his answer from the Father. His ministry, his sacrifice, will be for the heart; with no distinction of class, gender, race, or any other "natural" division — his Kingdom is to redeem the hearts of all (men and women, Jew and Gentile, slave and free) for all time.

Moreover, at the end of this story Jesus does not give her crumbs. He elevates her status in front of his disciples by declaring, "woman you have great faith!" Imagine what the disciples thought. Their Master's response takes them completely by surprise. It is as if Jesus is shouting, "Peter, look at this woman — she has great faith. She doesn't doubt." "My disciples, hear what I have to say, this woman has great faith. You want an example? Look at her. She is an example of great faith."

And he meets her need. "'Your request is granted!' And her daughter was healed at that moment" (v. 28). This encounter between the Canaanite woman and Jesus is unlike anything seen before or after. Do not misinterpret her actions. She is not groveling at the foot of some man, begging for scraps and willing to take the crumbs. This is only how it appears. Jesus reminds us that what is on the surface is meaningless; it is what is in our heart that touches God's heart. Jesus recognizes in her a faithful heart, which believes and does not doubt. He no longer looks at her "foreignness," her femaleness, her status; he looks solely at her heart — and it is great.

The Canaanite woman is a timeless role model for us. She is not like the bleeding woman who approaches from behind, hiding from view, or the crippled woman who stands far in the back of the temple and has to be brought forward. This woman shouts, confronts, impedes and falls down in worship. She is a grand, dramatic spirit; a courageous female who will do whatever she needs to do to gain God's attention — even without male permission, acceptance or approval. Even when it looks as if Jesus himself is not listening, she persists. She reminds God of his promises to the world. She is not begging out of ignorance. She is proclaiming her faith in the Messiah, in the riches of heaven open to those in need without discrimination. This person may be a heathen and a woman, but she accepts in her heart Jesus is "Lord, Son of David," and she comes to her Master's table with faith that mere bread crumbs will turn into twelve basketfuls. Therefore, they do.

~ ~ ~ ~ ~

MEDITATION

Consider Luke 18:1-8, the parable Jesus shares with his disciples about the persistent woman. She cries out for justice and does not give up. Jesus says, "will not God bring about justice for his chosen ones, who cry out to him day and night?" You may have heard you should ask God once and then accept your prayer as accomplished, but this parable and the example of the Canaanite woman indicate God responds to persistence.

Consider John 4:23. This scripture reveals how we are to worship God in spirit and in truth. Spend time worshiping the Lord without asking for anything. Bask in his glory.

Worship the Lord with gladness; come before him with joyful songs. — Psalms 100:2

Study Guide Questions

CANAANITE WOMAN

— List three things you want to remember about the Canaanite Woman.

— What does this story tell you about the mercy and compassion of God?

— Do you think as a daughter of God you have a right to be bold? Do you fear God's reaction? How does this story encourage you to boldly ask for what you need?

— How can you implement the promise of abundance in your life?

— What does this encounter reveal about the influence of women on Jesus' ministry?

— How is your heart before God? Have you been guilty of "going through the motions" in your faith? What do you need to do to change your attitude?

NOTES

XI

SAMARITAN WOMAN

The Samaritan woman's encounter with Jesus is only recorded in the fourth chapter of the Gospel of John, but their face-to-face exchange is the longest conversation between Jesus and another. The only other recorded conversation similar to this is when Jesus spoke to Nicodemus. Many compare the two and draw distinctive parallels and contrasts. My focus is strictly on the woman.

The Samaritan woman stands out as an important figure in the New Testament, particularly for women. This is a dialog between a man and a woman, between a Jew and a Samaritan, between the Son of God and a daughter of man. Imagine conversing this long with a woman. Imagine discussing theological issues with a woman. Imagine a woman converting practically a whole town by her testimony. It all happens in Sychar, Samaria, at Jacob's Well.

Jesus enters Samaria, the land of Gentiles, and sits at a well to rest while the disciples go into town to buy food. A woman comes to the well alone and Jesus asks her for a drink. Before long, they are conversing about politics, religion and spiritual matters. The conversation changes from a natural conversation to a supernatural experience as Jesus, speaking in the Spirit, tells her things about her life a stranger could not know. The woman is stunned, transformed and goes back into town where her testimony converts an entire town. It is an extraordinary event.

Please read their full conversation in John 4:4-42 before continuing this chapter. Because of its length, I separated this chapter into five distinct sections: dividing lines, intellectual discourse, gift of knowledge, worship, and evangelism.

DIVIDING LINES

The encounter between Jesus and the woman begins with John 4:4, "Jesus had to go through Samaria." This is a loaded statement. Most Jews who traveled north to Galilee go around Samaria, probably following the Jordan River. This makes for a longer journey, but most Jews went out of their way to avoid the Samaritans.

Why did Jesus have to travel through Samaria? There are only two possible explanations; he either is in a great hurry and must take the most direct route or — he has a divine appointment. There is no indication from the following scriptures he is in a hurry. He "had" to go through Samaria in order to meet this unnamed Samaritan woman who becomes a great evangelist.

To put their meeting in context, it is important to understand the setting. Samaria is situated between Galilee to the north and Judea to the south, between the Sea of Galilee and the Dead Sea. The trip is not long (about 35 miles), but it is full of hills and valleys. The city of Sychar is situated near the base of Mount Gerizim. Jacob's Well is located outside the city and is a welcome sight to weary travelers, including Jesus who stays there to rest while his disciples go into the city for food.

Among Biblical commentaries, there is some dispute as to whether

Sychar is another word for Shechem. A current theory is Sychar is the village of Askar, which is half a mile from Jacob's Well.[18] Since these two locations are within a couple of miles, more or less, of Jacob's Well, the distinction is not relevant to our discussion.

While his disciples go into town, Jesus sits next to this famed well. We can imagine he finds a spot of shade and sits, or perhaps leans back against the well to get comfortable, and ponders the history of the area. It is an ancient holy place, the birthplace of Israel.

Shechem is first mentioned in Genesis 12:6-7. "Abram traveled through the land as far as the site of the great tree of Moreh at Shechem... The Lord appeared to Abram and said, 'To your offspring I will give this land.' So he built an altar there... " After Abraham, the land passes to Isaac and then to Jacob. Jacob gives it as an inheritance to Joseph's two sons while they are living in Egypt (Genesis 48:21-22).

Four hundred years later, the Israelites, under Joshua, enter the Promised Land, make a covenant with the Lord, and "reclaim" the land — the land of Shechem. (Joshua 24:25) At Sychar, Joseph's mummy is entombed. In this same location, the kingdoms of Judah and Israel split apart. For millennia, the Israelites and the "Canaanites" have differed as to who "owns" the land — right up to this day. It is a holy land — a disputed land — and animosity, division, dispute, and much blood saturates its soil.

At the first mention of Jacob's Well (Genesis 29:1-3), we read the well is used by the "eastern people" to water their flocks. It is a deep well, kept pure by a large stone covering the opening. It must have been a huge stone because the shepherds had a standing rule to wait until all the flocks had arrived before they removed it to water their animals.[19]

It is at this well Jacob sees Rachel for the first time and falls in love with her. Even though not all the flocks have gathered, as soon as Rachel comes on the scene, Jacob moves the stone for her. They discover they are kinsmen and after fourteen years, Jacob finally wins his prize (after working for her father for seven years only to be wed to the older, nearsighted Leah, and then waiting seven more years before beautiful Rachel can be his). From Leah come eleven children, ten boys and a girl. From Rachel come Joseph and Benjamin. The twelve tribes of Israel originate from this chance encounter at the well. Jacob's bloodline goes through Judah, to David, to Jesus.

Do you think it is a coincidence Jesus meets a woman at Jacob's Well? It is where Rachel met Jacob, her kinsman and the ancestor of Jesus. Now Jesus meets a woman who implies she is his kinswoman (v. 12 "our father Jacob"). The implication cannot be clearer. This is a love story — not an earthly love like Jacob and Rachel's, but a spiritual love: the love of Yahweh for women. From this encounter, we are given a significant insight into how Jesus interacts with women; his acceptance, respect, empowerment, compassion and love for the marginalized.

Before we meet our Samaritan woman, let us find out more about the Samaritans. We have learned Jews disliked the Syro-Phoenicians, calling them "Canaanites," their term for Gentiles, but to call someone a "Samaritan" is an even greater insult. Why is there so much animosity between the Samaritans and the Jews?

This is a long story and starts at the beginning of the Biblical era. According to the Samaritans of Jesus' day, they are the children of Abraham, but the Jews do not consider them brothers — far from it. There are no more despised people than the Samaritans. Throughout their history when the Jews were favored, the Samaritans considered themselves Jews. But if the Jews were persecuted, the Samaritans embraced the persecutors and denied any connection.

The division began after the fall of Solomon's kingdom and the Israelites' split into the northern kingdom (Israel) and the southern kingdom (Judah). When Omri, king of Israel, comes to power, he establishes the city of Samaria (1 Kings 16:24). He is an evil king and those who come after him are even worse, blatant idol worshipers (like Ahab and his queen Jezebel, Ahaziah and Jehoram). The Samaritans, like the Jews, are dispossessed and taken into exile. Those who stay or eventually return to Samaria intermarry (and worship foreign gods whenever expedient) and to the Jews of the southern kingdom there is nothing "Jewish" about them.

In 538 BC, when the Jewish exiles return to rebuild their temple in Jerusalem they refuse the Samaritans' help (Ezra 4:1-5 and Nehemiah 4:2), so the Samaritans build a temple on Mount Gerizim.[20] The Samaritan woman refers to this temple in verse 20.

The Samaritans' religion has similarities to the Jews; they follow the Mosaic Law except they are perhaps more liberal in their beliefs, having been influenced by pagan thinking. They do not recognize any prophet after Moses. They observe the Jewish feasts and believe in, and long for, the coming Messiah.

Like the Jews at the time, their attitude toward women is drawn from a belief women are greatly inferior to men, a little better than animals. One thing is for certain, a man, whether Jew or Samaritan does not speak to a woman in public.

Now we have the background, let us return to the scene. Jesus waits at Jacob's Well while his disciples go into town to get food. Why is he alone? Is he so tired he cannot go with them? The scripture states he is "weary," but why does not one of his disciples stay with him to keep him company? We can assume Jesus sent them all away so he can meet this woman alone. He purposely waits for her. He has come for her.

While he is waiting, the woman arrives with an empty jug to draw water from the well. At a distance, she sees there is a man sitting by the well. She may have stopped and considered coming back later, but she has already traveled some distance. She must get her water.

The scripture states it is the "sixth hour." This detail is important because whether it is noon or six in the evening, women normally do not come to the well at either time. Drawing water and keeping a fresh water supply in the house is the role of women. Going to the well is probably a time of great social interaction; when women congregate, catch up on news and share information. I believe they would do this early in the morning when it is cool outside before their day begins. They will wait in line to draw water, so there are plenty of opportunities to talk with each other.

However, our Samaritan woman does not come when other women are around. She will be carrying a jug for water, balanced either on her head or in her arms, at the hottest time of the day. Why? We can imagine she has chosen this time of day because she is not likely to meet anyone. Either she has been ostracized or she has chosen to live outside the norms of Samaritan society. Whatever her reasons, she is a Samaritan who avoids other Samaritans — a person who is ranked pretty low. In fact, she might be considered the lowest of the low.

Jesus waits for this woman.

When she arrives at the well, Jesus asks her for a drink. He asks. He does not shout, so we know she has decided no matter who is sitting at the well, she is going to complete her task and comes forward. Perhaps she is already tying her line to her jug to draw out the water when he speaks to her. I see her. She keeps her head down, avoids eye contact, and tries to be as inconspicuous as possible. She sees he is a Jew, probably because he is wearing a tallit or a Jewish prayer shawl. She prepares for either abuse or avoidance. However, Jesus is no ordinary Jew.

"Will you give me a drink?" (John 4:7b)

Jesus does not say, "woman, give me a drink!" He asks. It is such a gentle request. In those few words, he conveys his love and compassion. It also shows respect, like a brother asking a sister or a father asking his daughter. It is not a request but a simple question. Because he asks, the woman is put in the position to refuse or accept. He empowers her. I am sure because he meets her in this way she has the courage to respond. But, according to the scriptures, she doesn't say "get your own drink." She says something quite unexpected.

"You are a Jew and I am a Samaritan woman. How can you ask me for a drink?" (v. 9) The first words out of her mouth declare the obvious division between them, Samaritan-Jew, male-female. She is confronted by two disturbing facts presented by Jesus' request for a drink; a Jew is speaking to a Samaritan and a man is speaking to a woman in public. Isn't it odd she feels the need to state the obvious? She does not like confrontation, but her first words are defensive. What is going on here? She is puzzled and wondering, "how can he not know that I am a Samaritan woman and he, a Jewish man?"

As a person who has suffered from societal separation, she still feels the need to declare the "truth" of their differences. She has learned to accept the "fact" she is the lowest of the low. Society has defined her. An age-old division of nationality and gender — over which she has no control — separates her. Through no fault of her own she is on the wrong side of the dividing line.

Jesus answers her question with the most remarkable statement. "If you knew the gift of God and who it is that asks you for a drink, you would have asked him and he would have given you living water" (v. 10).

Isn't it amazing how Jesus does not respond by acknowledging manmade divisions? He goes directly to the heart. "If you knew the gift of God... you would have asked and he would have given..." In Matthew 7:7, Jesus reiterates this point, "Ask and it will be given to you; seek and you will find; knock and the door will be opened to you." Even though she immediately acknowledges the gulf between them, Jesus bridges the gap by revealing the heart of God. She will never be the same.

INTELLECTUAL DISCOURSE

What is this gift of God Jesus offers? The Greek word for gift, *dorea*, denotes it is a free gift. To what free gift of God is Jesus referring — the gift of eternal life, the gift of the Holy Spirit, the gift of salvation, the gift of love, peace, or joy? Yes, all of these. However, the gift Jesus is referring to in this passage is himself. He is the gift of God (John 3:16), and through him all these other things are added, coming from and through him. In other words, he might have said, "if you knew me, you would know I am here for you. Nothing can separate us."

It is not what he says that is remarkable, but that he says it at all to this Samaritan woman. It is profound Truth. Jesus is the "living water." He imparts to this ostracized, lowly woman the greatest truth God has for us.

What makes him say this to her? He could have said, "you're right, I am a Jew, but I'm thirsty; be so kind as to give me a drink." Jesus knows the heart of God and he knows this woman's heart. He soon demonstrates he knows more about her than anyone else does. He knows as soon as she comes to the well what kind of woman she is, how she is living and what her thoughts are. He can see how hungry, desperate, sad, and lonely she is. He knows all too well how man's laws have separated her from God's plan. He makes this profound statement to her because He knows she will receive it.

She does receive it; only she takes his words literally and eagerly engages him further with her questions. She must be quite excited he is willing to respond kindly to her.

"Sir," the woman said, "you have nothing to draw with and the well is deep. Where can you get this living water? Are you greater than our father Jacob, who gave us the well and drank from it himself, as did also his sons and his livestock?" (vv. 11-12)

Through her words, she is trying to show him she is a follower of Yahweh, and she holds to the old ways and knows her history. Remember, Samaritans are viewed as a shifty lot who follow whatever religion is expedient; many of them worship idols and most likely, at that time, worship Roman gods. Those who still follow the Mosaic Law are more like Sadducees. However, this woman feels compelled to share with Jesus she knows her Jewish roots, the story of Jacob and the well.

In answer to her question "Where can you get this living water?" (John 4:11b), Jesus responds with the greatest love story ever told: "Everyone who drinks this water will be thirsty again, but whoever drinks the water I give them will never thirst. Indeed the water I give them will become in them a spring of water welling up to eternal life" (vv. 13, 14). The free gift of eternal life through Jesus Christ is the gospel message.

Still thinking in natural terms, the Samaritan woman begs him in verse 15, "Give me this water, so that I won't get thirsty and have to keep coming here to draw water. (i.e. have to be humiliated by coming alone at noon to avoid the townswomen)" Her eager response reveals even more that she is hungry for a solution to her problems. Do you think anyone else has ever offered her such a gift? There is something about Jesus that makes her immediately accept his wild claim that he has water for those who wish to never thirst again.

Because of her questions, I can imagine she is intelligent. Her mind may be thinking; "if I have this water, I can be independent. People will come from miles around for my water. I will not have to come to this well again. The other women will come to me for my living water."

GIFT OF KNOWLEDGE

The Samaritan woman does not yet know to whom she is speaking. She does not know Jesus is the Son of God, the promised Messiah. But Jesus knows what she's thinking ("If you knew the gift of God and who it is that asks you for a drink... " v. 10) He may be wholly man, weary and hungry as he is at that moment, but he continuously operates in the supernatural. All the gifts of the Spirit are available to him. In this instance, he uses the gift of knowledge. He can see the wheels turning in her head, see she is thinking in natural terms; she is missing the point. He puts an end to all that when he says, "Go call your husband and come back" (v. 16).

He already knows she doesn't have a husband. He is waiting for the opportunity to bring her practiced dissembling into a more personal encounter. His statement brings her back to her reality, to her lowly condition. Her fantasy of becoming important and accepted through earthly means dissipates in an instant as she is confronted with her secret sin.

In verse 17, she carefully admits this but neglects to reveal the full truth. She says, "I have no husband." (Notice she does not call him "sir," showing how rattled she is.) He is a stranger. He will not know she is living with a man who is not her husband. In his presence, she feels compelled to tell the truth but not the whole truth. She does not want to see the disgust in his eyes or be rejected by him if he knows the truth about her. She thinks she can deceive him with clever words.

Note how Jesus responds to her statement. It says so much about how we are to interact with people who suffer under guilt. There is nothing condemning in his words. He demonstrates his power through the gift of knowledge, which makes it impossible for her to hide her shame. He gently removes her mask.

"You are right when you say that you have no husband. The fact is, you have had five husbands, and the man you now have is not your husband. What you have just said is quite true" (vv. 17, 18). In other words, "good for you for not lying to God. He knows your life and sees your heart." He reveals her secret sin but compliments her on being truthful. It is so kind, so loving, and so powerful. She is astounded. This Jewish man, this stranger, knows intimate details of the shameful life she has been leading.

Much has been made of the Samaritan woman's checkered past — some say she is at worst a prostitute or at best a woman of low morals. She has had five husbands and now lives with a man to whom she is not married. She brazenly speaks with a Jewish man in public — alone. She debates theology with him. She has an inquisitive attitude. She brings a whole town to the Lord.

The Samaritan woman has been characterized differently by theologians throughout the ages, coloring her by the prevailing attitude toward women of their time. Because her story is in the Gospel of John, and her conversation with Jesus is both lengthy and revealing and conveys foundational spiritual truths; it is impossible to leave it out. She must be addressed. Since her story is relevant no matter what century, we in the 21st century can bring our own prevailing view of who she is as a woman.

From our point of view, she is way ahead of her time, a modern woman. She has married and divorced five times before she ends up living with a man (not that multiple marriages make her modern, but it does show us she's unconventional for the time; many women today opt to live with a man outside of marriage). She is not an adulteress or she would have been stoned five times over. She is a divorcée. We don't know why she has been divorced so many times, but we know at that time women could not divorce their husbands, so there is something about her which makes the men in her life discard her.

Given the kinds of questions she asks Jesus, it is reasonable to assume she is a woman of considerable intelligence and curiosity, a woman who speaks her mind and doesn't wait to be given permission by men to speak, a woman who likes to engage in theological debates, a nonconformist. This would have made her a woman men of that time could not abide.

That she was married five times also indicates there is something greatly attractive about her. She must be an extremely beautiful or sensual woman who, despite her previous relationships, is still desirable to men — four men, at least, married her knowing she was not a virgin.

We do not know anything about her live-in boyfriend, but we know he is not a devout or honorable man; otherwise, he would have married her. He may be a Greek who does not see the need to marry a Samaritan; or she may be the mistress of a Roman officer stationed in Samaria. This might be the reason she avoids the censure of the townspeople. The Romans are an occupying force and a woman who lives with one would be an outcast. We do not know who he is. We only know the Samaritan woman does not acknowledge his existence to Jesus. This is a woman who has been unlucky in love five times and no longer cares whether she is married or not. Her life cannot be easy.

So many women today are like this woman. They look to a man to provide for them through marriage without understanding the sacredness of the marital union, only to have that relationship end in divorce and disillusionment, leaving them worse off, and older, than before. Bitterness replaces optimism. Scheming replaces genuine affection. They compromise and settle for a relationship that does not honor them. They live with the shame of abandonment, the fear of loneliness and the regret of past mistakes.

With each successive bad relationship, the Samaritan woman's self-esteem diminishes; her value decreases. That she has been married five times reveals a life of constant shame, disappointment, heartache and grief.

However, because of the way she engages Jesus in conversation, I see her also as a strong woman, a woman with a voice, and one who pushes the edges of conventions. I like this woman. Jesus likes this woman; I know this because he does not give up on her. He graciously converses with her despite conventions.

But, more than that, Jesus imparts to her deep spiritual Truths about the Kingdom of God, the nature of God, and the way to worship God. He knows he's talking to a Samaritan woman, but he doesn't say to her, "these matters are too weighty for a mere woman to understand" or "if you were a man, I'd explain it to you, but since you are a woman there is no need."

He does not tell her to shut up and get him the water he asked for. He does not talk down to her. He patiently listens and responds to all her questions. He bestows incredible honor on her. He has compassion for her. He treats her like an equal, with no condemnation, no disgust, and no admonition to change her ways, no patronizing tone.

As stunned as she is by his uncanny knowledge of her secrets, she has an immediate and intelligent response:

> "Sir," the woman said, "I can see that you are a prophet. Our ancestors worshiped on this mountain, but you Jews claim that the place where we must worship is in Jerusalem" (vv. 19, 20).

By calling him a prophet, she acknowledges his accurate depiction of her life, perhaps to flatter him or to show him honor. In one powerful sentence, she raises the greatest controversy and antagonism between the Jews and the Samaritans. She is practically challenging him to explain this age-old division between their people. This subject is worthy of intellectual debate.

WORSHIP

In true apologetic fashion, she lobs at him the Samaritans' number one controversy — the true place of worship. It is as if she has participated in or heard many discussions regarding this subject and is ready to argue her side. Leave it to Jesus to see through her ploy to move the conversation away from her personal life and onto a more controversial subject, one in any other circles would cause a flurry of discussion and intense argument.

Because the Samaritans do not acknowledge any prophets beyond Moses, their "worship" is not only incomplete but also centers on empty rituals of sacrifice. The location of these sacrifices is the temple on Mount Gerizim. Jesus is not taken in and vanquishes the controversy on both sides, revealing the heart of God.

> "Woman," Jesus replied, "believe me, a time is coming when you will worship the Father neither on this mountain nor in Jerusalem. You Samaritans worship what you do not know; we worship what we do know, for salvation is from the Jews. Yet a time is coming and has now come

when the true worshipers will worship the Father in Spirit and in truth, for they are the kind of worshipers the Father seeks. God is spirit and the true worshipers must worship in spirit and in truth" (vv. 21-24).

It almost makes me cry to hear his response to her. All the division between people that man creates is swept away by his words: "true worshipers will worship the Father in Spirit and in truth — for they are the kind of worshipers the Father seeks." Jesus is saying all the rituals and laws of the Samaritans and the Jews will be replaced by worship through the Holy Spirit and those who accept the gospel message will become "true worshippers."

In one fell swoop, he demolishes the man-made laws that divide men and women, Jews and Gentiles, religions and denominations. Worshipping God has nothing to do with earthly rules, laws and locations — it is through the Spirit. What is more, God seeks true worshippers whether Jew or Gentile, man or woman, old or young.

These verses are explosive and foundational to our understanding of the Father. "God is a Spirit." God is not inanimate like an idol. God is alive. He is omniscient, omnipresent and omnipotent. He is the Creator of all things. He is not an impersonal being. He loves his creation. He is active. He "seeks" true worshipers. He chooses to engage with human beings and has spoken to people throughout time. God is invisible, not visible to our human senses, even though He manifests in the physical through various means (i.e. a burning bush, a dove, a cloud).

God is Spirit. He must be worshiped in spirit and not through meaningless rituals or sacrifices, but from the spark of God within us. This is at the root of man's misunderstanding of God's heart. We want to do something to prove our faith. We go to church, read our Bibles, sing songs of worship, and do good deeds. All these things are good, but they do not please God in and of themselves. True worship comes from our spirit; when our hearts and minds are focused solely on God for no other purpose than to love and praise him.

EVANGELISM

Jesus' response again stuns her. I am sure she does not understand it, but she does deduce from this "prophet" it has something to do with the Messiah. She says, "I know that Messiah (the Christ) is coming. When he comes, he will explain everything to us" (v. 25). Even though the Samaritans do not recognize any prophet beyond Moses, she and her people have an understanding from the Mosaic tradition there is a Messiah who will come. That she calls Jesus a prophet in the first place shows she is acknowledging the possibility he is the Messiah, but she does not know this consciously. She is in the presence of the Messiah (although she doesn't realize it) and faith is manifested in her spirit.

> Then Jesus declares, "I, the one who is speaking to you
> — I am he" (v. 26).

To this woman, he declares himself as the promised Messiah. Whatever thoughts she has been having during her conversation with Jesus, wondering who he is; he now leaves no room for doubt. He says it straight out. There is only one other passage during Jesus' ministry where he directly states his divine nature (John 8:58). He certainly implies it in Luke 4:16-21, when after he has been tempted in the wilderness, he enters the synagogue in Nazareth and reads specifically a passage from Isaiah 61:1-2 regarding the coming Messiah and declares, "today this scripture is fulfilled in your hearing" (Luke 4:21).

He does not correct those who call him the Christ or the Son of God (He does; however, admonish them not to tell anyone). In Matthew 16:16 when he asks his disciples "who do you say I am," Peter replies "You are the Christ," and Jesus responds that the Father revealed this to Peter. He then orders his disciples not to tell anyone. Jesus does not openly state he is the Messiah; he allows others to declare it (See Matthew 14:33, John

1:29, John 1:34, John 1:49, John 6:69, John 11:27). In John 8:58, Jesus comes the closest to stating he is the Messiah when he says, "Before Abraham was born, I am." This drives the Jews into frenzy and they pick up stones to kill him for blasphemy.

Nevertheless, in the case of the Samaritan woman, Jesus tells her straight out he is the Messiah, "I am he" (John 4:26). Before she can even respond to this remarkable declaration, the disciples return and are shocked to see him conversing with a Samaritan woman. From the scriptures, we gather unlike her they do not ask him any questions, but their disdain is obvious. I do not think the woman even notices. She has heard Jesus say he is the Messiah. She takes the opportunity to become an evangelist — she runs to tell her townspeople she has met the long-awaited Messiah; at least she believes she has.

"Come, see a man who told me everything I ever did. Could this be the Messiah?" (v. 29)

We can forgive her tentative testimony because she is new to evangelism and she is facing a town full of people who have reviled or ostracized her for years. Will they believe her? Will they think she is crazy? She is so filled with zeal she persists in telling them about her encounter with Jesus. Her question, "could this be the Messiah?" does not come from a lack of faith, but from a sense of awe and wonder — and hope.

There is another aspect to her statement that is interesting. She says Jesus "told me everything I ever did." All that is recorded is that Jesus reveals he knows about her four husbands and live-in companion. That is certainly not "everything" about her life but it is all we hear. This suggests that they had an even longer conversation in which Jesus tells her things about herself no one could know.

What is also interesting is she takes "on faith" his claim to be the Messiah. Even if she thinks at first he is a powerful soothsayer or fortune-teller, at some time during their conversation she begins to believe he really is the Messiah. Most likely, this occurs when he reveals that God knows her heart; he knows her guilt, her longing, her frustration, and her need. I have no doubt through him she receives forgiveness and becomes a "new creature." The Spirit of the Living God touches her. She is transformed.

While she is away beginning her evangelizing, the disciples try to get Jesus to eat, but he refuses, saying, "I have food to eat that you know nothing about." They ponder this, thinking someone, perhaps this woman who left when they arrived, gave him food to eat. At that moment, Jesus is full. He is full of the Holy Spirit and joy in seeing the transformation of this unfortunate woman.

He goes on to talk to them about "the harvest," which is another word for evangelism. Even though he does not speak of the woman specifically, he is definitely aware she is in Sychar evangelizing and at that moment the townspeople are coming out to meet him. Souls are ripe for the harvest and the disciples, who have nothing to do with sowing the seed, will reap the harvest.

> Jesus says to them, "Open your eyes and look at the fields! They are ripe for harvest. Even now, the one who reaps draws a wage and harvests a crop for eternal life, so that the sower and the reaper may be glad together. Thus the saying 'One sows and another reaps' is true. I want you to reap what you have not worked for. Others have done the hard work, and you have reaped the benefits of their labor" (John 4:35-38).

"Others have done the hard work," meaning the Samaritan woman has done the hard work, facing a skeptical, even hostile, town full of people and telling them about the man at the well who can read her thoughts. She might even have conveyed his startling words that neither Mount Gerizim nor Jerusalem is the only place to worship God and "true worshippers" worship in Spirit and in truth. Whatever she tells them, the scripture states "many believed in him because of the woman's testimony" and a considerable crowd comes out of Sychar to see Jesus and beg him to stay with them (John 4:40).

Jesus says to his disciples in John 4:36, "Even now the one who reaps draws a wage and harvests a crop for eternal life, so that the sower and the reaper may be glad together."

To whom is he referring? He is referring to the Samaritan woman. Through her evangelism, she is drawing a wage and harvesting a crop for eternal life. And the sower (Jesus) and the reaper (the woman) will be glad together. Jesus is "glad" and is making a specific point to his judgmental, chauvinistic disciples. He noted their shock and disgust when they saw him talking to the Samaritan woman.

The woman's testimony is so powerful many believe in Jesus based on listening to her. This tells us she says more to them than "He told me everything I ever did." It also tells us given her propensity to talk and ask questions, she must be a persuasive speaker.

As laywomen, it is important for us to follow her example. Your testimony is a powerful means of sharing the gospel. You do not need to be a Biblical scholar, minister, or Christian leader to share your own personal story about how Jesus changed your life. Sharing the gospel through your testimony can bring thousands of people to Christ.

Empowered by the Holy Spirit, your words can make an impact. If you are not comfortable in explaining Christian theology, fearful you do not know enough about the Bible to refute well honed and logical arguments, you can simply rely on the power of your own personal testimony.

In this, you are an expert. In this, you can count on the Spirit of the living God to give you the words to pierce the heart of the unbeliever. Remember the Samaritan woman. She is the lowest of the low, rejected by her peers, silenced by her culture, isolated by her sin, yet through her testimony a whole town comes to know about Jesus.

~ ~ ~ ~ ~

MEDITATION

Jesus is always willing to hear from us. He is waiting for us to talk to him. How do you do this? Begin by worshipping him, either through songs of praise or expressions of gratitude and thanksgiving.

Clear your mind of your thoughts and plans and wait to hear what he has to say. He may tell you about everything you ever did, or he may tell you something unexpected.

Draw near to me and I will draw near to you. — *James 4:8*

I love those who love me, and those who seek me find me.
   — *Proverbs 8:17*

Study Guide Questions

SAMARITAN WOMAN

— List three things you want to remember about the Samaritan Woman.

—Why is the location at Jacob's Well significant?

— What have you learned about Jesus from this story?

— What did the woman say to the townspeople to bring them to the well to see Jesus? What is your testimony? Briefly share it with the group.

— What is Jesus referring to regarding sowing, reaping and harvesting for eternal life?

— What have you learned about true worship?

— Have you or other women you know been discouraged by a lack of leadership opportunities in your church? Discuss how Jesus' encounter with the Samaritan woman addresses this issue.

NOTES

XII

SISTERS: MARTHA AND MARY

Martha and Mary are sisters who live with their brother Lazarus in Bethany, a couple of miles from Jerusalem. They are early disciples and great friends of Jesus. There are three accounts in the Bible of these famous women, primarily because Jesus loved to be around them. Their stories are familiar to us: 1) Martha upset when Mary does not help her because she is at Jesus' feet, 2) Lazarus dies and is raised from the dead by Jesus, and 3) Mary breaks an expensive jar of ointment (spikenard) to anoint Jesus before his death.

Luke's is the only Gospel that records the first story; John's is the only Gospel that records the second. All four Gospels record the third, but only Luke credits Mary of Bethany as the woman who anoints Jesus. These encounters are powerful, giving us a picture of Jesus' heart toward the sisters in particular and women in general.

This close-knit Jewish family is important to Jesus, and his interaction with them is unlike any other recorded in the New Testament. They love him, and he loves them. These three examples reveal a close bond among them, like a second family. We know Martha is in charge of the household, so she is either a well-to-do widow or the eldest daughter whose parents are dead, leaving her responsible for the care of her younger siblings. Mary is younger and Lazarus is a sickly individual (he is not mentioned in the first account).

When Jesus comes into Martha's life, she finds a friend closer than a brother. These are not romantic feelings, but there is definitely something special between them and a deep personal friendship develops. Their relationship is unique in the scriptures. It is mature and based on mutual respect. Jesus imparts to Martha deep spiritual truths which she comes to accept and believe.

Mary's relationship with Jesus is more spontaneous, more child-like, but his love for her is undeniable; he is as close as a brother.

The first mention of Martha and Mary is in Luke 10:38-42:

LORD, DON'T YOU CARE?

"As Jesus and his disciples were on their way, he came to a village where a woman named Martha opened her home to him. She had a sister called Mary, who sat at the Lord's feet listening to what he said.

But Martha was distracted by all the preparations that had to be made. She came to him and asked, 'Lord, don't you care that my sister has left me to do the work by myself? Tell her to help me!'

'Martha, Martha,' the Lord answered, 'you are worried and upset about many things, but few things are needed — or indeed only one. Mary has chosen what is better, and it will not be taken away from her.'"

We should not be surprised this story of Martha and Mary is controversial. It is filled with dualistic imagery. Every woman who hears this story reacts to it differently. Some love it. Some hate it. Some draw great truth from it and others walk away confused. This face-to-face encounter with the Savior is a message about and particularly for women. It is important to come to terms with this message and see past any disagreement to understand our Savior's heart.

These two women of Bethany represent two significant and different aspects of a woman's character — the practical and the spiritual. Both are important, but one is considered "better" than the other. According to Jesus, seeking the Kingdom of God always takes precedence over earthly matters. It is not that Mary is "better" than Martha, but her choice to seek God first is preferable to Martha's more practical choice to tend to Jesus' and his disciples' needs.

This is not merely a female inclination; it is a human tendency. Throughout the scriptures, Jesus exhorts his disciples and the listening crowds to put God first. Let us look at how Jesus elaborates along these lines in Matthew 6:31-34:

> "So do not worry, saying, 'What shall we eat?' or 'What shall we drink?' or 'What shall we wear?' For the pagans run after all these things, and your heavenly Father knows that you need them. But seek first his kingdom and his righteousness, and all these things will be given to you as well. Therefore do not worry about tomorrow, for tomorrow will worry about itself. Each day has enough trouble of its own."

As humans, we live in a world requiring us to care for our loved ones, to provide food and shelter, to work for a living. It is easy and natural for us to believe we are on our own in the struggle. Nevertheless, the truth is our Heavenly Father knows what we need. If we put him first, we will receive "all these things." The direction here is simple — sit at the feet of Jesus and receive his blessing.

Martha first meets Jesus when he is at her door. She graciously opens her home to him and his disciples (we don't know how many there are with him, but we will assume only the twelve). She "opened her home"; it is not her brother's or Mary's home. She has the authority to invite Jesus to visit and stay with them without seeking the approval of someone else. So it is reasonable to assume Martha is in charge of the household. From this first encounter, Jesus becomes the family's close friend, often stopping to stay at Martha's house — which is always open to him.

In verse 40, we learn Martha is making "all the preparations that had to be made." What are these preparations? We do not know. We can imagine inviting thirteen people to stay will be an ordeal requiring quite a bit of organizing and preparation. Moreover, since one of her guests is the famous rabbi claimed by some to be the Son of God, she wants to make a good impression. We can be sure she is organizing a big welcoming feast for sixteen people at minimum. There is even the possibility she is responsible for finding places for them to sleep, washing their clothes, or even arranging for them to take baths. All we learn from this scripture is Martha is extremely busy and there are many things to do.

It is important for us to put Martha in the proper light. The Greek word for Martha's distracted mental state is *periespato*, which also translates as "perplexed" or "pulled in two different ways at once."[21] She is not *periespato* because she is busy for the sake of appearances but because she is doing everything she can to provide for Jesus' comfort. Her concern is for the Lord.

We must not make the mistake of thinking Martha is somehow carnally inclined in her preparations. She is simply giving in her service to Jesus. And although Jesus says Mary has "chosen what is better," it does not mean he is denigrating Martha's kind and necessary actions. As usual, our Lord is imparting a deep spiritual truth from the most mundane and ordinary circumstances. All our efforts, no matter how well intentioned and righteous, can't compare to the simple act of sitting at the feet of Jesus, learning and receiving unmerited favor from our Lord. It is that simple.

Still, as Martha prepares things for Jesus' comfort, she eventually notices her sister is nowhere to be found and when she discovers Mary sitting in the room with all the men listening to Jesus' words — at his feet no less — we can understand why she is upset. Her sister is not only leaving all the work for her to do but is sitting in the coveted spot at Jesus' feet. After all, it was Martha's idea to invite Jesus. She probably wishes she were at his feet listening to his words as Mary is (and probably her brother, Lazarus, even though he is not mentioned in this passage), instead of working. However, someone must take care of the necessities when guests arrive.

You can picture Martha running around arranging things, excited that Jesus is in her home, catching snippets of what he is saying. It thrills her to her soul. She hears the disciples asking questions and Jesus' responses. What he says penetrates her heart. He is unlike anyone she has ever known. Since she has honored him with her hospitality, opening her home to him and his disciples, she has obviously heard him before and seen the results of his healing ministry. Perhaps he will heal her little brother Lazarus. He is a great rabbi and he heals all who come to him. Perhaps this is why she invited him in the first place.

I believe at this first encounter Martha does not know Jesus is the Christ (because of the way she speaks to him). He is a great teacher, probably a prophet, certainly a celebrity, and her honored guest. It thrills her to be able to care for him in her home — if there were not so much to do — and where is her sister?

She glances into the room and there is Mary, sitting at the rabbi's feet as if she has nothing to do — no responsibility. You can imagine Martha's shock, frustration and jealousy, as she speaks in exasperation to Jesus, "Lord, don't you care that my sister has left me to do the work by myself? Tell her to help me" (v. 40b).

"Lord, don't you care…"

What a thing to say! Don't you care? How many times do we think Jesus does not care about our circumstances? This is how we all are sometimes — overwhelmed by details, aware of all that needs to be done while those around us appear clueless, concerned about the future, overworked and underappreciated, treading water and losing energy fast — thinking no one cares. If not for us everything will fall apart. We carry a heavy load.

> "Come to me, all you who are weary and burdened, and
> I will give you rest." — Matthew 11:28

"Lord, don't you care?"

Martha has every right to feel this way. As a woman living 2,100 years ago, before the redemption of Christ, responsible for her brother and sister, she is unappreciated and must navigate hostile waters in a society that does not make it easy for a woman — and she has only one person to rely on — her younger sister Mary.

Let us think about where Martha is when she accuses Jesus of not caring. (I do not think she means it as an accusation.) She is in her own home, probably in the largest room of the house where all the men are sitting, lounging, being refreshed and fed by her generosity. She sees Mary boldly sitting at the Lord's feet, paying close attention. She is exasperated. Does she shout from the doorway? I don't think so. She will not want to embarrass her guest or draw attention to Mary's laziness. She will probably come to Jesus' side and whisper loud enough for Mary to hear.

I can see Jesus smiling, knowing what is in Martha's heart, loving her, and wanting to impart something important to her. He looks up into her face; knowing she is expecting him to agree with her, and says, "Martha, Martha, you are worried and upset about many things, but few things are needed — or indeed only one. Mary has chosen what is better, and it will not be taken away from her" (v. 41).

Jesus repeats Martha's name as a sign of endearment, intimacy, and friendship. He tells her she is concerned about many things, but "few things are needed…" In other words, as much as he appreciates her efforts, she is going above and beyond his expectations. He requires only a little food, a little water, and a place to lay his head. She has taken it upon herself to define his requirements to demonstrate how much she honors him. This is so human — so female. He did not ask for a fuss to be made over him. He will be quite satisfied with a drink and a loaf of bread with Mary and Martha at his feet, listening to his words.

Because she is so much like us, we can forgive Martha for not understanding. No matter how deeply we understand God's grace, we still feel obligated to do something, perform, shine — exceed all our own expectations to win God's approval. It is the natural state of mankind, separated from God by sin. Not until Jesus paid our debt in full through his blood on the cross did we stand before God without condemnation.

This is such a powerful truth, and again, Jesus imparts it to a woman — to Martha, whom he loves.

Imagine Jesus saying to you, "You do not need to impress me. I am right here. Those who find me I will not send away. Come, sit, and rest at my feet. Make me your priority and do not worry about other things."

AT THE LORD'S FEET

In the following encounter, Martha's heart is changed. She becomes a believer in Jesus as the Christ. Mary changes as well.

> "She [Martha] had a sister called Mary, who sat at the Lord's feet listening to what he said." — Luke 10:39

Mary sits on the floor at the Lord's feet — at the feet of the famous rabbi. This privilege is reserved for male Jewish scholars or students of the Law — never a woman. This is well known at the time.

This important concept can be more fully understood through an example of the Apostle Paul. When Paul is accused of starting a riot and arrested, the Roman commander gives him permission to address the Jews who want to kill him. Paul tells the angry mob he is a Jew who has studied at the feet of Gamaliel (Acts 22:3). This information has a profound effect on the crowd. Gamaliel is a famous and revered rabbi, a powerful leader of the Sanhedrin. Paul knows by saying he studied "at the feet" of Gamaliel, he will be seen as a man of importance with great credibility.

Jesus is now most likely inside Martha's house with his disciples, talking and sharing, and it is obvious Mary is out of place in this room full of men. When Martha raises this point to Jesus, he admonishes her and says Mary has "chosen what is better." It is "better" that she is at his feet, listening to his words.

By choosing "what is better," Mary violates all the social and religious norms of her culture and her time. Women do not mingle with men, particularly single women. Women do not engage in theological discussions because they are thought incapable of understanding. Women's roles are well defined, and Mary is violating them. I don't know if the disciples are by now accustomed to Jesus ignoring gender distinctions, but there must be a few eyebrows raised when Mary comes in and sits at Jesus' feet; presumably she is the only female in the room.

One explanation is she is a young woman, somewhat naive and innocent, completely without guile and endearing to everyone she meets. Perhaps no one has the heart to tell her she can't sit at Jesus' feet. It is, after all, her house and the Master, their guest, does not seem to object. Even when the elder sister comes in and reminds Jesus that Mary is not helping, not fulfilling her household obligations, he refuses to send her off to carry out her duties, as defined by her gender. Instead he says, "Mary has chosen what is better, and it will not be taken away from her" (v. 42).

The story ends there. We do not hear anything from Mary. She must have been speechless. I am sure she feels some guilt for leaving all the work to Martha, but she is so captivated by Jesus she has no other thought than to be with him. She must know her action will cause a stir, but she feels comfortable with Jesus and his disciples.

When he absolves Mary and says he will not send her away, I can imagine she falls in love with him on the spot. Here is a famous man, a learned rabbi, who respects her as a person — someone with value. He allows her to sit at his feet. He compliments her, saying she has chosen wisely. He will not deny her the right to seek the kingdom of God. He elevates her in the presence of her sister and his own disciples.

She probably is in awe and it may not be her nature to ask questions, but we find in later scriptures that this Mary is not averse to showing her feelings. Martha, on the other hand, is more complicated. Even though she respects and loves Jesus, she cannot help but feel he has let her down, particularly when her brother Lazarus dies. How can she not, but she does not yet know Jesus can conquer death.

LORD, IF ONLY. . .

> "Now a man named Lazarus was sick. He was from Bethany, the village of Mary and her sister Martha." (According to John's Gospel, this Mary, whose brother Lazarus now lies sick, is the same one who poured perfume on the Lord and wiped his feet with her hair.) "So the sisters sent word to Jesus, 'Lord, the one you love is sick.' " — John 11:1-2

This second encounter of Jesus, Martha and Mary is recorded only in John's Gospel (John 11:1-45). When Jesus raises Lazarus from the dead, he does so in front of a large crowd of mourners. Word travels like wildfire and quickly reaches the ears of the chief priests and synagogue rulers who begin to plot Jesus' death. In their corrupt minds, it is one thing to claim you are the Son of God, but when you convince people you have the power to raise people from the dead, you must die.

At the beginning of this story (John 11:2), John indicates a third encounter with this Mary who will anoint Jesus before his death (John 12:1-9). Because John's account differs from the other three Gospels regarding this anointing, I have addressed the third encounter separately from the stories of sisters Martha and Mary (see Chapter 13, The Anointing Woman).

In John 11:3, the sisters send word to Jesus that their brother is sick. "He whom you love is sick." What a simple prayer request, and yet it is so effective. Martha and Mary only remind Jesus of his love for Lazarus, and therefore they have full faith he will come and heal their brother. They only have to say, "he is sick," and Jesus will know what to do. This is how close their relationship is. There is no begging or pleading, no detailed explanation of what is wrong with Lazarus, only that he is sick and is loved. "Come quick!" is implied in the message, but so is their faith. Because Jesus is now practically a member of their household, they know he will not disappoint them. So what happens? He arrives too late. At least this is how it appears.

We can take heart from this. When we send our urgent prayer to the Lord, we can be assured he hears us, but we must then exercise our faith and believe the prayer will be answered according to his will and his timing, not ours. We do not have the full information or see the hand of God. We must trust and believe. Even if we do not get an immediate response does not mean God has not heard us. Sometimes God tarries with his answer for a better result. This is something we must take on faith.

Jesus does not rush to Bethany to heal his sick friend. Instead, he purposefully stays away two more days. He explains the delay will be "for God's glory so that God's Son may be glorified through it" (v. 4). He knows Lazarus is mortally ill. Perhaps he has known for some time that Lazarus has a fatal illness. When he receives word Lazarus is sick, he knows his friend is facing death. But he waits until Lazarus has died before going on to Bethany where he will perform the miracle of miracles — he will raise Lazarus from the dead and in so doing provide a concrete example of his power over death.

Jesus is fully aware that coming near Jerusalem is extremely dangerous. As his disciples point out to him, the Jews there want to kill him (v. 8). When he tells his followers Lazarus is dead, Thomas bravely says, "Let's go and die with him" (vv. 14-16). But this is not a story about death. It is a story about life eternal. Jesus finally arrives in Bethany. Lazarus has died and has been entombed for four days.

> "When Martha heard that Jesus was coming, she went out to meet him, but Mary stayed at home. 'Lord," Martha said to Jesus, 'if you had been here, my brother would not have died. But I know that even now God will give you whatever you ask.' Jesus said to her, 'Your brother will rise again.'
>
> Martha answered, 'I know he will rise again in the resurrection at the last day.' Jesus said to her, 'I am the resurrection and the life. The one who believes in me will live, even though they die; and whoever lives by believing in me will never die. Do you believe this?' 'Yes, Lord,' she replied, 'I believe that you are the Messiah, the Son of God, who is to come into the world.' "— John 11:20-27

It is so like Martha to confront Jesus with an uncomfortable truth. "Lord, if you had been here, my brother would not have died." While Mary stays at home, probably inconsolable with grief, Martha stoically overcomes her own grief and runs to meet Jesus before he arrives in town.

However, this is not the same Martha who had complained she was not getting the help she needed. She has grown tremendously. Even though she is a practical woman, she has become deeply spiritual. She makes it clear right at the beginning that she believes Jesus has the power to heal her brother. She believes in his supernatural gifts. Then she makes the most amazing statement of faith: "I know that even now God will give you whatever you ask" (v. 22).

Can she possibly believe Jesus will raise her dead brother from the grave? She knows God will give Jesus whatever he asks, and if he asks God to restore her brother, it will be done. However, this is personal, not intellectual

Sometimes we can believe for others, but are not able to believe for ourselves. It is too much for us to expect Jesus' supernatural powers to defeat death. We know Martha does not yet have full understanding of his power because at Lazarus' tomb she warns him not to open the tomb because her brother's body will surely stink from decomposition (v. 39). Her statement, however, indicates she has faith in God. Jesus knows her heart. He understands her struggle to believe that heaven has actually come to earth.

Jesus replies, "Your brother will rise again" (v. 23).

The practical Martha acknowledges the current pharisaic belief that there is a resurrection of the dead. Perhaps she replies without thinking about it, not knowing how to respond to Jesus' assurance that Lazarus will arise. She wants to believe, but how can she? Her brother has been dead for four days. Then what Jesus says next penetrates Martha's heart and soul.

> "I am the resurrection and the life. The one who believes
> in me will live, even though they die; and whoever lives
> by believing in me will never die. Do you believe this?"
> — John 11:25-26

Martha says unequivocally, "I believe." She is no longer spouting religious platitudes. She is expressing her true faith. She no longer believes Jesus is a great rabbi. She experiences the power of the Holy Spirit within him and knows he is truly the Messiah.

She throws away her doubt, even in the face of her beloved brother's death, even in the face of her own grief and practical frame of mind. Standing next to Jesus, face-to-face, seeing his love for her and hearing his Spirit-filled, powerful words, she believes at her core that he is, as he says, the resurrection and the life. Her spirit leaps within her:

> "I believe that you are the Messiah, the Son of God, who
> is to come into the world" — John 11:27.

You can tell Jesus is deeply moved by this encounter with Martha. He must have thought about it while he was purposefully tarrying before walking toward Bethany. He tells his disciples plainly that Lazarus is dead… "and for your sake I am glad I was not there, so that you may believe" (v. 15).

He knows he is going to bring his good friend Lazarus, the brother of Martha and Mary, back to life. He knows Martha and Mary are deeply grieved. He knows his own death is imminent, and his resurrection will once and for all atone for mankind's sin and set them free to be in relationship with God. More than anything he wants these three dear people, his faithful disciples and his followers, to understand and believe that as the Son of God he conquers death. If Lazarus can come back from the dead after four days, Christ can and will return after three days in the tomb. It will soon come to pass.

All this may be in his mind as he nears Bethany. He is prepared to experience the great grief in Martha's household, but she surprises him by meeting him on the outskirts of town. I think she catches him off guard. I think this is why he loves Martha so much — she is unpredictable, passionate, and earnest. Her love for him is unmistakable.

When he says Lazarus will rise again, and he sees the pain of loss on Martha's face, and hears her spout a half-hearted belief in the resurrection of the dead; he proclaims the greatest Truth of all time: "I am the resurrection and the life. The one who believes in me will live, even though they die; and whoever lives by believing in me will never die. Do you believe this?" (vv. 25-26).

This is Jesus' question to Martha. It is God's question to us. Martha says, "I believe."

After she says she believes him, she rushes back to her house and finds Mary. She says, "The Teacher is here." She does not say, "Mary, Jesus the Messiah is here." I do not believe this is a lack of faith. They probably refer to Jesus as the "teacher" or "rabbi" when they talk about him. It shows respect and is a familiar designation.

Even though Mary is grieving inside the house alone (in some translations she is "still" as if paralyzed), she rushes out to meet Jesus who is walking with Martha. When she reaches him, she immediately says the same thing Martha has said. It is as if the two have discussed it many times between themselves. She also professes her belief that if Jesus had been there to heal Lazarus, their brother would not have died. There is no doubt she is inconsolable.

We know this because of Jesus' reaction to her in John 11:33-35.

> "When Jesus saw her weeping, and the Jews who had come along with her also weeping, he was deeply moved in spirit and troubled. 'Where have you laid him?' he asked. 'Come and see, Lord,' they replied.

> "Jesus wept."

This is the heart of Jesus. This is our Savior. This is the one to whom we take our troubles when we are grieving, upset or facing a difficult challenge. This is the one who wipes away our every tear. This is the one who is deeply moved by us.

When he sees their grief he is deeply moved and "troubled." Some translations state he "groaned" or "wept." These are important passages. Jesus experiences the deepest of human emotions and empathizes with those he loves.

When we are troubled in spirit, we can know when we pray we are speaking to one who has wept with us, for us, and is able to conquer all our fears, tears and grief.

From that point, Jesus immediately goes into action. He is taken to Lazarus' tomb, thanks God and calls Lazarus to come out of the tomb. Practical Martha worries his corpse will smell, and Jesus admonishes her to stand on her words of belief. Lazarus comes out wrapped in strips of linen with his face covered. It is a miraculous moment and many Jews believe Jesus is the Messiah.

This encounter with Martha and Mary is even more powerful because we know they are good friends. As phenomenal and spectacular as this resurrection is, it is clothed in a poignant human setting of relationships among four people.

Because of Martha and Mary, we have a picture of Jesus both human and divine. He interacts with patience, humor, compassion, and emotion. He is both humble and supreme. By entering into the lives of Martha, Mary and Lazarus, Jesus becomes real and believable. If you think Jesus is a great man or a spiritual teacher, you are not accepting the full account. He proves to his friend Martha that he is not only a great rabbi but also the long-awaited Messiah, the Son of God with the resurrecting power of the Holy Spirit.

> "Father, I thank you that you have heard me. I know that you always hear me, but I said this for the benefit of the people standing here, that they may believe that you sent me." — John 11:41-42

~ ~ ~ ~ ~

MEDITATION

Jesus wept. He felt all human emotion, sorrow, sadness, confusion, fear, hope against hope, and deep familial love. When we come to our Savior, we are not coming to someone who has no idea what it is like to be human. He knows. He cares for you.

The Word became flesh and made his dwelling among us. We have seen his glory, the glory of the One and Only, who came from the Father, full of grace and truth. — John 1:14

Study Guide Questions

SISTERS: MARTHA AND MARY

— List three things you want to remember about Martha and three things you want to remember about her sister, Mary.

— How does the story of these sisters inform your understanding of Jesus' view on women in ministry and in domestic roles?

— Discuss what it means that Jesus allows Mary to sit at his feet in a room full of men.

— The relationship Jesus has with Martha and Mary is one of friendship. Why is it important to see Jesus as a friend? Read John 15:13-15 and discuss what this means.

— Why did Jesus wait a few days instead of leaving right away when he learned Lazarus was dying? What can we learn from this?

— Jesus raised Lazarus from the dead. What in your life is impossible, beyond your ability to change? Do you believe Christ can change the situation? Discuss what we can learn from Martha's faith to believe in Christ's resurrection power.

NOTES

XIII

ANOINTING WOMAN

"And I tell you this in solemn truth, that wherever the Good News is preached throughout the world, this woman's deed will be remembered and praised." — Mark 14:9 (TLB)

I begin this chapter with Jesus' own words because the woman who anoints his feet is remembered for our spiritual benefit. Jesus is so moved by this woman's act he says, "this woman's deed will be remembered and praised." Jesus memorializes this woman and makes sure no matter what things are later recorded about him, this woman and her act of love and worship will be remembered.

The story of the woman who anoints Jesus is repeated and repeated and recorded in each one of the Gospels. Matthew's and Mark's words are almost identical in their portrayal of the incident. A woman anoints Jesus and all four Gospels record it.

The story is essentially the same in all the Gospels, but the setting changes somewhat, the woman's identity is uncertain and the method of anointing varies. Jesus pronounces a command that her story not be forgotten — and it isn't — but the name of the woman has been erased from all but John's account. He identifies her as Mary of Bethany, Martha's sister (John 12:2-3).

The other Gospel writers do not identify her by name. They call her "woman" or "sinner." Five hundred years later, Pope Gregory I (AD 540-604) will identify her as Mary Magdalene and infer she was a prostitute (how else would she have expensive spikenard ointment and use it so shamelessly?). Because of what is said in Pope Gregory's Homily 33, the Catholic Church disseminated the notion that Mary Magdalene was a prostitute. This belief held fast for fourteen hundred years until 1969 when the Catholic Church disallowed it.[22] However, this fallacy is still believed and taught today in some churches (See Chapter 15 on Mary Magdalene).

The central story is essentially this: Jesus is reclining at dinner when a woman enters, breaks open an alabaster jar and uses an expensive perfumed oil to anoint him. Jesus' companions are upset over the waste of precious ointment but he chides them, telling them she is anointing him for his burial and she will be remembered for her act.

I will use Matthew's version because it is the shortest, but you will want to look at the other Gospels to get a fuller picture of this encounter (Mark 14:3-9, Luke 7:36-50 and John 12:1-8). Our goal is not so much to reconcile discrepancies, as it is to gain a better understanding of how Jesus interacts with this woman. Let us examine in Matthew 26:6-13 what Mary does and the ways we can learn from her:

> "While Jesus was in Bethany in the home of Simon the Leper, a woman came to him with an alabaster jar of very expensive perfume, which she poured on his head as he was reclining at the table. When the disciples saw this, they were indignant. 'Why this waste?' they asked.

'This perfume could have been sold at a high price and the money given to the poor.'

Aware of this, Jesus said to them, 'Why are you bothering this woman? She has done a beautiful thing to me. The poor you will always have with you, but you will not always have me. When she poured this perfume on my body, she did it to prepare me for burial. Truly I tell you, wherever this gospel is preached throughout the world, what she has done will also be told, in memory of her.'"

Let us put this story, which varies slightly in each author's account, into context. Jesus is in Bethany (v. 6), three miles from Jerusalem. This is the same town where Martha, Mary and Lazarus live. It is a safe haven for Jesus before entering Jerusalem, as we have come to see by reading about Martha and Mary. All the Gospels, except Luke (who gives no location), agree on this fact. It is a story told repeatedly. People remembered this incident. The details may be lost in the retelling, but its essence has been preserved for all time.

Jesus goes to the home of Simon the Leper, where he will probably spend the night. We can assume Simon is someone who has been touched and healed by Jesus and has become one of his followers. It is doubtful people will dine with someone who still suffers from leprosy. Luke tells us this person is a Pharisee named Simon. Simon the Leper is a Pharisee. John's Gospel is different; Jesus is not at Simon's house but at Martha's home, where her sister Mary also lives.

In John's Gospel, it is six days before Passover, barely a week before Jesus is crucified. In Mark's Gospel, it is only two days before his death. Jesus refers to this anointing as a preparation for his burial, even though his disciples do not fully understand what is soon to take place.

Mark indicates it is because of this "wasteful" incident that Judas Iscariot loses his respect for Jesus and goes to the chief priests to make a deal to betray him. Judas appears furious that Jesus defends the actions of this "sinful" woman. In a fit of righteous indignation, Judas determines Jesus is a fraud and he is done with him — all because of this woman and her costly perfumed ointment.

What is the significance of this anointing? In the Old Testament, those who are "anointed" are elevated to rulers or kings. Think of Saul and how Samuel anoints him as the first king of Israel (1 Samuel 10:1). Think of David and how Samuel anoints him as king (1 Samuel 16:13), and how David will not kill Saul because he is God's "anointed" (1 Samuel 24:6).

The word "Messiah" means "the anointed one." Jesus is our high priest and our king. This woman's act of anointing Jesus is not only to prepare him for burial (as he states), but also to declare him Messiah and king. She recognizes him as the Messiah. Moreover, in this role, she serves Jesus as a high priest would. I know many will find this assertion controversial. How could this person, this woman, possibly be considered a high priest?

This is the only recorded incident where Jesus is anointed with oil as befits a king — and Jesus commends this woman for her actions, memorializes her for it, because it is right that he be anointed as King of the Jews. It doesn't appear to matter to him that it is a woman who anoints him.

> "But you are a chosen people, a royal priesthood, a holy nation, God's special possession, that you may declare the praises of him who called you out of darkness into his wonderful light." — 1 Peter 2:9

In Mark 14:8, Jesus explains that the woman has anointed him for his burial. Did no one hear his words? They do not want to think about death or the end of their time with Jesus. Whether they acknowledge it or not, Jesus is about to be killed and this woman who is moved by the Holy Spirit has anointed him for burial.

In Luke, the explanation is slightly different. Jesus describes the anointing as an act of love, honor and hospitality. In Luke 7:44b-46, Jesus explains:

> [Addressing Simon] "Do you see this woman? I came into your house. You did not give me any water for my feet, but she wet my feet with her tears and wiped them with her hair. You did not give me a kiss, but this woman, from the time I entered, has not stopped kissing my feet. You did not put oil on my head, but she has poured perfume on my feet."

Another important point to be made is her actions are almost identical to foot washing and may possibly have given Jesus an idea. Shortly after this incident, before his betrayal, Jesus washes the feet of his disciples' feet (John 13:1-17). In verses 14-16, he says:

> "Now that I, your Lord and Teacher, have washed your feet, you also should wash one another's feet. I have set you an example that you should do as I have done for you. Very truly I tell you, no servant is greater than his master, nor is a messenger greater than the one who sent him."

In other words, the woman who kneels at his feet, washes them with her tears and dries them with her hair serves as an example for the disciples. Jesus reminds them that this woman who received their disdain and umbrage for her actions is to be emulated. Jesus, in his earthly ministry, continually turns things around and breaks stereotypes through his words and his actions.

Let us enter Simon the Leper/Simon the Pharisee's home where this unusual, controversial, and memorable act of anointing takes place. Jesus is relaxing, reclining at a table and eating with his host and disciples. A woman suddenly appears and in dramatic fashion throws herself at

Jesus' feet, crying copious tears, so much so that she wipes them away with her hair, which is long and loose. All the while she is kissing his feet. She breaks open an alabaster jar of expensive oil she has brought and pours it on Jesus' feet. If we examine this scene, we can understand why it causes such a stir. It is unprecedented. It is shocking. The woman must be out of her mind.

What is even more shocking to observers is Jesus placidly continues to recline and allows her to anoint and kiss him. According to all the writings on this, he does not sit up and object, "Please don't do that, it's inappropriate," or "Stop! It is not right for a woman to touch a man who is not her husband in that way!" No, Jesus is at ease.

Let us see it from the woman's point of view. Even though we do not know exactly who she is, we can assume somehow she has heard that Jesus is staying in Bethany. Determining which home he is visiting, she grabs her alabaster jar of nard and runs through the streets to the house. She does not bother to bind up her hair or cover it. She does not want to miss seeing him. She cradles the jar in her arms, knowing her plan of action will raise eyebrows. Jesus' companions may not allow her to see him. She does not care. She is driven, compelled to follow an inner feeling to anoint Jesus.

She enters the house — whether she is a harlot or Martha's sweet sister Mary — with no invitation, no introduction. She comes in quickly so no one will deter her, determined to do what she has come to do. She has obtained this oil at great expense, perhaps with her own future burial in mind. In each of the Gospel accounts, you realize this woman is not to be denied. She breaks open the seal on the alabaster jar of pure nard and immediately begins to anoint Jesus' head and feet.

In Matthew and Mark, she pours the scented oil on his head, which in most translations is called nard, but in Mark, Jesus states she also anoints "his body" (Mark 14:8). In Luke 7:38, "she began to wet his feet with her tears. Then she wiped them with her hair, kissed them and poured perfume on them." In John 12:3, Mary "poured it on Jesus' feet and wiped his feet with her hair."

No matter which version you read, and despite the discrepancies, the action is more or less the same — a woman uses expensive perfumed oil to anoint Jesus in the presence of many men, an action considered extremely intimate.

In most translations, the word for the oil is spikenard (*Nardostachys jatamansi*), shortened to "nard", one of the most expensive oils or ointments of the time. It is extremely fragrant with a musky, pungent aroma. It originates from a plant of the valerian family with rose-purple flowers, cultivated in the hills of the Himalayas — far from Jerusalem.

Even in those days, nard had to be transported from India into Persia, then to Rome. The oil extract is derived from the tuberous root of the plant in a time-consuming distillation process. A derivative of the herb valerian, it produces a calming effect when applied. Nard's scent was equated with the fragrance of the Garden of Eden and the substance was highly prized.[23] The Romans greatly valued it, and it was, according to John's account, "worth a year's wages." It was the best anointing oil to be had. There is only one other place in the Bible that refers to nard — the sensuous and beautiful Song of Songs, a love poem. Spikenard is associated with marriage and erotic love:

> While the king sitteth at his table, my spikenard sendeth forth the smell thereof. A bundle of myrrh is my well beloved unto me; he shall lie all night betwixt my breasts." — Song of Songs 1:12-13 (KJV)

> "You are like a lovely orchard bearing precious fruit, with the rarest of perfumes; nard and saffron, calamus and cinnamon, and perfume from every other incense tree, as well as myrrh and aloes, and every other lovely spice." — Song of Songs 4:13-14 (TLB)

Let us not shy away from this picture of erotic love between a man and a woman — in perfect union. It is a picture of the beloved wooed by his bride — her perfume filling the room — and of the bride being loved and cherished by her bridegroom. As physically arousing as it appears, the sensuality is intentional and serves as a metaphor for Christ's relationship with his church —bridegroom and bride. It is intimate — a relationship with no equal. It is the perfect union of the physical and the holy, as it was supposed to be in the Garden of Eden — God and his creation. As hard as this is to comprehend, Jesus wants this kind of relationship with you — a perfect union.

You can see why there is such outrage by those attending Jesus in Bethany.

Who is this woman, really? How does she come to have such expensive perfumed oil in her possession? In Matthew and Mark, she is unnamed, but obviously, she has means enough to own an alabaster jar of precious nard. In John, she is Mary, the sister of Martha and Lazarus; which might indicate they had nard left over from when they had prepared Lazarus' body for burial. We do not really know where she got the perfume. We know only she has it and has made an independent decision to use it to anoint Jesus. No matter how the story is told, this singular fact remains.

In Luke 7, she is known as "the woman in that town who lived a sinful life" (v. 37). This is quite a contrast — is this virtuous Mary of Bethany who sits at the feet of Jesus? Or a different woman of questionable morals, perhaps even a prostitute? When we look at all of the Gospel references together, we can only account for this discrepancy by seeing it from a feminine perspective. A woman who is so brazen as to use expensive nard (associated with erotic love) to anoint a stranger's feet must be either a virtuous saint or a prostitute.

Simon the Leper thinks to himself, "If this man were a prophet, he would know who is touching him and what kind of woman she is — she is a sinner," (Luke 7:39) but Jesus, knowing Simon's thoughts, responds with a parable about "someone" (gender unspecific) who suffers from a large debt.

> "'Two people owed money to a certain moneylender. One owed him five hundred denarii, and the other fifty. Neither of them had the money to pay him back, so he forgave the debts of both. Now which of them will love him more?' Simon replied, 'I suppose the one who had the bigger debt forgiven.' 'You have judged correctly,' Jesus said. 'Therefore, I tell you, her many sins have been forgiven — as her great love has shown. But whoever has been forgiven little loves little.'" —Luke 7:41-43, 47

I include these passages because they speak volumes about how Jesus sees women. Simon sees her as someone lacking virtue, a sinner, a prostitute, but Jesus sees her as she is — a child of God, his beloved. He recognizes what she did was done out of love for him. He states unequivocally, "as her great love has shown." He enumerates her loving actions, contrasting them to Simon's lack of action. He knows her heart. She worships him. Jesus is greatly moved and wants her actions to be remembered and replicated forever.

This passage is for all women. Even when they are reviled, put down, dismissed, and devalued, Jesus raises women up and recognizes their acts of worship and love. He understands from a man's point of view (his disciples', Simon's, Judas Iscariot's) the woman behaved improperly and her actions are deemed wrong and wasteful, but from God's point of view, the woman rightly obeys the Lord's call.

According to the scriptures, and by the nature of the perfume, the fragrance fills the room. Even those not paying attention to the woman's entrance with an alabaster jar will immediately become aware of the fragrance filling the room. All conversation stops as people look in shock at what is going on. There at the feet of Jesus is a woman kneeling, anointing him, using her hair to wipe his feet. Or there, behind him, is a woman who is crying and combing the expensive oil through his long hair with her fingers. No matter which version, this act is so intimate, so precious, it is hard to describe in mere words.

If, as Jesus explains, she is anointing him for his burial, this is an act reserved for the closest female relative; a mother, sister, wife, or daughter. Here is this woman who is not related to him, anointing him in this ceremonial yet familiar and intimate way. The men in the room are quite uncomfortable. Jesus seems to be enjoying the ritual, so they cannot chastise her for her familiarity.

Every Gospel indicates a gut reaction to the woman's act. No matter who speaks it, the men in the room are shocked. They go for the one thing — the expensive nard, which could have been sold instead and the money donated to those in need — they are sure will be seen as sensible. What a waste of money. How dare this woman waste a year's wages on a single act when she could have sold it and given the money to the poor. They know Jesus hates wastefulness and how the rich ignore the plight of the poor

The disciples feel quite self-righteous about castigating this woman for her flagrant waste. You can imagine how it is with the twelve, and all the followers; how they want to be acknowledged by Jesus, recognized for being one of the "in crowd," among Jesus' intimates, better, smarter, holier than others. They vie for his attention and approval. They angle to show how "holy" they are.

Once again, Jesus pulls the rug out from under this self-righteousness. Rather than see the woman's act as one of immense love and worship, they see it as wrong and wasteful. Jesus puts them straight. "Leave her alone. Why are you bothering her? She has done a beautiful thing to me... She did what she could. She poured perfume on my body beforehand to prepare for my burial." (Mark 14:6, 8).

In Luke 7:48-50, Jesus continues the discussion, one of which has already ended in the other three Gospels. It is important to include it because he speaks to the woman in Luke's version:

"Then Jesus said to her, 'Your sins are forgiven.' The other guests began to say among themselves, 'Who is this who even forgives sins?' Jesus said to the woman, 'Your faith has saved you; go in peace.'"

REMEMBER HER FOR THIS

This woman who anoints Jesus follows God's instruction; follows her faith and ignores all the societal restrictions, indignation and ridicule, rejection by the community, and her fear of being made to look a fool. She obeys the Holy Spirit who galvanizes her to go to Jesus and properly anoint him before his death. Jesus immediately sees her actions as an act of faith. He also sees a fearless act of great love. He forgives her sins (whatever they may be) and causes the guests in Simon's house to wonder who he really is.

Consider this: Jesus is relaxing at the table when this wild-haired woman comes in to anoint him. He recognizes her as having been sent by the Holy Spirit and allows her to anoint him, liberally and intimately. From my point of view, there is nothing more pleasurable than being massaged with oil. The sensation of another's hands rubbing and touching the skin with oil is relaxing and peaceful.

She may also have poured it slowly over his head, running her fingers through his hair to distribute the oil. (If you have ever had a scalp massage you know how relaxing it is.) The woman uses her own hair to wipe away the excess oil. This is a sensuous act, full of ardor and love, bringing a tickling, tender, stimulating feeling. The smell fills the nostrils and the fragrance conjures up images of flowers, tree bark, hillsides, the forest, the Garden of Eden — and brings a sense of wholeness; a feeling of being in harmony with God and without sin.

Everyone present can smell the pungent perfume. It is tempting to imagine what they experience when they sniff the scent of spikenard. For some, it may be the first time; it is both precious and expensive. Others may have smelled it in the boudoir of a courtesan. Some may remember it from the laying to rest of a loved one.

And when she is finished, and Jesus has given her his blessing and forgiveness, he says to everyone there: "And I tell you this in solemn truth, that wherever the Good News is preached throughout the world, this woman's deed will be remembered and praised." The woman who anoints Jesus is remembered to this day.

Jesus wants us to remember her, not only because she anointed him for his burial; but also because of who she is and what she did as her act of faith, love, and worship. She gave no thought to the value of the perfume. She gave her best. She gave no thought to herself. She heard the call of God, she answered, and she had peace in her heart.

It is my hope we will see from her example that no matter what walls are put up to keep women out, if the Lord calls your heart, you will obey him rather than the law of man, and that you will risk ridicule and censure to obey God. It is this intimate relationship he wants with you, in which he speaks to your heart and out of your love, you hear his voice and follow.

If you are called to "anoint" someone for prayer or for worship, obey Shekinah, the Holy Spirit. If you are gifted with wisdom and knowledge, obey the Shekinah and speak out. If you are chosen or "anointed" as a leader, obey Shekinah. Be a woman who anoints.

~ ~ ~ ~ ~

MEDITATION

One of the most beautiful and poetic books of the Bible is the Song of Songs, which illuminates and honors human sensuality. It is passionate and graphic, celebrating the intimate love between a man and woman.

From this and the story of the anointing woman, we see God loves his creation — both its physical and spiritual aspects.

Anoint your skin with scented oil and luxuriate in the awakening of your senses. As you rub the oil into your palms, inhale deeply and thank the Lord for your physical being. Thank the Lord for making you female. Honor and celebrate your life. Meditate on how Jesus thoroughly enjoyed and honored what the woman with the alabaster jar did for him. You can enjoy your life. You can celebrate your body — as it is.

... as a bridegroom rejoices over his bride, so will your God rejoice over you. — Isaiah 62:5b

You love righteousness and hate wickedness; therefore God, your God, has set you above your companions by anointing you with the oil of joy. — Psalm 45:7

Study Guide Questions

ANOINTING WOMAN

— List three things you want to remember about the Anointing Woman.

— Which version of this story in the Gospels is your favorite and why? Who do you think the anointing woman is?

— What is the woman's purpose in anointing Jesus? Is she anointing him for burial, as Jesus says, or did she perhaps have another purpose in mind?

— Why is anointing so powerful? Share a similar experience you have had and the result.

— Discuss what you think it means to be of a "royal priesthood" as stated in 1 Peter 2:9. How will this impact the way you see yourself?

— Does the sensuality of this story give you a new perspective of Jesus? If so, discuss how your perception has changed.

NOTES

XIV

WANTON WOMAN

There is no more poignant story of Jesus' interaction with women than his encounter with the woman caught in adultery, probably because this story reveals in stark contrast Christ's grace over man's law. It is remarkable that it begins with such viciousness and concludes with forgiveness triumphant — and in the middle of it all is a woman.

This nameless woman caught in the act of adultery stands alone, condemned and reviled by society and is used as an unwitting pawn to trap Jesus. She does not commit adultery alone, but she stands alone and faces death alone. Everyone is against her — men, women, priests, society, and the Mosaic Law. The only one on her side is Jesus.

The story is told in John 8:2-11:

> "At dawn he appeared again in the temple courts, where all the people gathered around him, and he sat down to teach them. The teachers of the law and the Pharisees brought in a woman caught in adultery.

They made her stand before the group and said to Jesus, "Teacher, this woman was caught in the act of adultery. In the Law, Moses commanded us to stone such women. Now what do you say?" They were using this question as a trap, in order to have a basis for accusing him.

But Jesus bent down and started to write on the ground with his finger. When they kept on questioning him, he straightened up and said to them, "Let any one of you who is without sin be the first to throw a stone at her." Again he stooped down and wrote on the ground.

At this, those who heard began to go away one at a time, the older ones first, until only Jesus was left, with the woman still standing there.

"Jesus straightened up and asked her, 'Woman, where are they? Has no one condemned you?' 'No one, sir,' she said.

'Then neither do I condemn you,' Jesus declared. 'Go now and leave your life of sin.'"

There has been much written on this story so I do not want to cover the same ground as more eminent scholars and teachers. My hope is new revelation will spark our understanding of how Jesus deals with, interacts with and understands women through this story.

We have seen in many earlier passages how compassionate our Lord is to widows. The culture of the time was often unfair to them. Without their husbands or a male heir, a widow was pitiable, stripped of all rights and dependent on the charity of others unless she had independent means. Jesus deplores this situation; the hard-heartedness of his people and the desperation of the widows break his heart. However, as cruel as this practice is a widow is still respectable and honored.

There is another kind of woman who fares far worse — she is the independent single woman or, as some might say, a wanton woman.

In a culture where women have no value except for their functional sexuality — whether as whores or mothers — women who are unmarried with no family and no resources have few options. Many end up bartering their bodies for their livelihood. Unfortunately, many nations and cultures devalue women. They are objectified for their ability to procreate or give men sexual pleasure. They are not seen as people but as objects.

This ploy of the devil must be defeated at all costs. As Christian women, when we are confronted with women being viewed, displayed or treated like property or objects, we must speak against it. Satan wants to destroy women and keep them from their inheritance. Remember the creation story when Adam and Eve eat the apple and their eyes are opened. God asks Eve, "What have you done?" and she says: "The serpent beguiled me, and I did eat." God curses Satan for what he did to Eve in an interesting way:

> "I will put enmity between you and the woman, and between your offspring and hers; he will crush your head, and you will strike his heel." — Genesis 3:15 (KJV)

From the beginning, there has been enmity between women and Satan. It is no coincidence that here in the 21st-century women still struggle to claim their full inheritance as children of God. In his infinite wisdom, God devises a plan through Eve (woman) to redeem the world — through an offspring who will crush Satan's power — Jesus the Messiah!

Today, we see this enmity revealed in advertisements, songs, films, television and other visual media. Women and girls are under siege. Too often they are represented in a sexual context. It permeates our culture. I am frequently shocked to find how many young women accept and promote this lie. Those who push back against this cultural tide are often dismissed, ridiculed, or labeled as a "feminist". Women in the church may not face the same sexual objectification, but their gender is often used against them to keep them out of the pulpit.

The truth is the spirit within women — the holy spark of creation — and the longing of their souls puts them on equal footing with men. Women may be physically different from men, but their human desires, failings, and intellect are the same. They are not of less value than men. In the eyes of God, they are his precious, beautiful creation — his children.

This accused adulteress who is publicly humiliated represents women's carnal nature exposed to the light of day. Is this wanton woman a prostitute? Most scholars believe she is. We do not really know. All we know about her is she is caught in the act of adultery (not fornication, which is the sexual act). Adultery means she is either having sex with a married man or she is married or engaged to be married. Either way, according to Mosaic Law her actions are considered worthy of a death sentence.

What is most surprising about the Pharisees' crafty plan to trap Jesus is during this time adultery is so common it is rarely prosecuted. Mosaic Law does not indicate stoning as the punishment for infidelity. Rather, the woman is to be stoned if she is betrothed (Deuteronomy 22:23). It is possible that this is the case since the plan was to catch Jesus countermanding the Mosaic Law. Perhaps the adulteress is not a prostitute, but a woman betrothed.

Noted Bible scholar and Methodist theologian Adam Clarke (1762-1832) spent forty years writing a commentary on the Bible, which has served as a primary resource for more than two centuries. His commentary on John 8:2-11 states some early Catholic writers known as Popists believed this adulteress to be Susanna who was espoused to an old, impotent man named Manassah.[24] (Susanna is mentioned in Luke 8 as one of the female disciples and followers of Jesus. See Chapter 16 on Women Disciples.)

Remember, Jesus' mother, Mary, was in a similar situation — she was betrothed to Joseph and was pregnant. According to Mosaic Law,

Mary should have been stoned to death.

Let us go even further. Perhaps this wanton woman is not a prostitute as most Bible scholars assert, but a divorced woman. How many women today fit into the category? I do. I have great empathy for this woman. I did not want a divorce, and it continued to affect my life for decades. Because of my education, legal rulings, and societal acceptance, I fared much better than this woman of the first century. Think about how many times the subject of divorce came up with Jesus, even though he is not the one who brings it up. The leaders of Mosaic Law, the Pharisees, and Sadducees, find it one of their favorite topics of debate.

In Matthew 19:3 and Mark 10:2, the Pharisees came to Jesus to test him and asked, "Is it lawful for a man to divorce his wife for any and every reason?" At this time there were two schools of thought on the question of divorce — one was a man could not legally divorce his wife unless she was unfaithful, and the other was a man could divorce his wife for any reason, even if he simply saw someone he liked better or his wife burned his bread. This heated debate polarizes the religious community. It is the perfect question to snare Jesus in their trap.

To add to our understanding we need to read where this practice originated. It comes from the ancient Mosaic Law in Deuteronomy 24:1-4:

> "If a man marries a woman who becomes displeasing to him because he finds something indecent about her, and he writes her a certificate of divorce, gives it to her and sends her from his house, and if after she leaves his house she becomes the wife of another man, and her second husband dislikes her and writes her a certificate of divorce, gives it to her and sends her from his house, or if he dies, then her first husband, who divorced her, is not allowed to marry her again after she has been defiled."

In Luke 16:18, in response to the hard-heartedness and self-righteousness of the Pharisees, Jesus upends the law on divorce and instead of blaming women, calls men to account, "Anyone who divorces his wife and marries another woman commits adultery, and the man who marries a divorced woman commits adultery."

Think about this for a moment — based on the Law, a man can divorce his wife for "displeasing him" or for finding "something indecent about her." It is not difficult to see how after a thousand years, this law is given liberal interpretation and is widely applied. Women are extremely vulnerable. It is quite unlikely they are divorced virgins. After being married, a woman is no longer considered chaste but is now defiled. And as she grows older, particularly if she has not produced a child, she may be "displeasing."

What would you do if you were divorced in the first century? If like the Samaritan woman you are able to capture the interest of a man and remarry, you will have means of support. However, if you are unable to marry again, how will you support yourself? With legions of Roman soldiers looking for sex, it would be a struggle to maintain your virtue when facing starvation. Regardless of this woman's true status, this is a mean-spirited scenario used to catch Jesus — probably the easiest to come up with and the easiest to execute.

Before he goes to Jerusalem where he will meet this woman, Jesus is staying in Galilee. His brothers tell him he needs to leave because it is getting too hot for him there — people want him dead. While his brothers go on to Jerusalem for the Jewish Feast of Tabernacles, Jesus stays behind (John 7:1-5).

The Feast of Tabernacles is a weeklong festival, known as Sukkot, which celebrates the Israelites' 40-year journey in the wilderness and the success of the harvest. All Jewish males are required to appear at the Temple in Jerusalem. Therefore, this is a time when the temple is filled with men. It is a celebration as a reminder of God's protection, provision, and faithfulness.[25] Even though it is a religious festival and a holy day, there will be a lot of carnal activity. Prostitutes or loose women will be in great demand.

Midway through the festival, Jesus travels secretly to Jerusalem. Even though he knows there is a plot to kill him, he is able to enter the temple courts without detection. The scriptures say there is already quite a lot of gossip and rumor about him, and everyone is wondering where he is. When he begins teaching, he is immediately surrounded. His detractors confront him and shout that he is demon-possessed (John 7:20).

Even so, people begin to believe he is the Messiah. This is not what the Pharisees want. Every time they try to expose him as a fraud it backfires on them. Even the temple guards sent to arrest Jesus return without him. The chief priests are furious and alarmed when their own guards become convinced Jesus is a holy man. It drives them into a murderous frenzy. They must find another way to silence him — and quick.

On the last evening of the festival, Jesus leaves this super-charged atmosphere and heads for the Mount of Olives to find rest and peace. At dawn, he returns to the temple and begins to teach again in the courtyard. As usual, a crowd surrounds him. It is most likely he is in the Court of Women or the Outer Court, because the Jewish leaders bring the wanton woman to face him and she would not be allowed in the Court of Men — but remember, at this time, the weeklong festival has concluded and the temple is filled to capacity with Jewish men.

Jesus sits while he teaches. This is his way. He gets comfortable with the people, possibly both men and women, although it is doubtful many women are there at this time. He is not standing on the steps preaching or otherwise attracting attention to himself. He is keeping a low profile. This is only about six months before his crucifixion. Once people know where Jesus is, they come in droves. His words, his actions, his spirit draw or repel people like a super magnet. They hang quietly on his every word, so the only sound besides the hustle and bustle of temple life is the sound of Jesus' voice.

Then in the distance there is a ruckus — the sound of a woman screaming and men shouting. Soon the disruption breaks into the courtyard and a half-naked, struggling woman is pulled in front of Jesus. We do not know what the woman is wearing, if anything. We do know from scripture she is caught "in the very act" so she may be naked, half-naked, or wearing disheveled, torn clothing. Her hair is most likely loose, another sign of her wantonness, and she probably has red marks on her arms and legs from being dragged roughly through the streets. Men either hold her in place or she stands by herself, surrounded and weak with defeat. There is nowhere for her to run.

Not until Jesus speaks to her does she say anything, at least nothing is recorded. Where does this woman come from? How do the chief priests and Pharisees know where and when to pick up this woman "in the act" to use in their plot against Jesus? She probably knows one of them; maybe she is someone's lover, maybe her espoused has complained to the priests, maybe she is a known prostitute used by the temple priests. Any number of scenarios are possible.

With all these people surrounding her, the real question is where is the man? He is not identified or mentioned. If this woman was caught "in the act," then a man must have been with her. Why was he not brought before Jesus for judgment? There is every chance he is in the crowd, and he is probably already armed with a stone and calling for her death.

"Teacher, this woman was caught in the act of adultery.
In the Law, Moses commanded us to stone such women.
Now what do you say?" (John 8:4-5).

This is the set-up. It is well planned and well-timed. The Pharisees appear to know this woman. Perhaps one of their own has arranged to meet with her. How else would they know when and where to grab her "in the act"? They drag the woman who has been caught in the act of adultery (with verifiable evidence from several eyewitnesses) to the temple courts where they know Jesus will be.

They quote the Law of Moses and then demand Jesus publicly respond to their accusations. If he declares she should be stoned, they can and will report him to the Roman authorities for rendering a death sentence, which is Rome's right, not the Jews'. But if he says she should be let go and not put to death, they will have proof he opposes the Mosaic Law and not a true prophet. They will loudly declare him to be a fraud. It is a neat trick. The chief priests, scribes, and Pharisees must think themselves quite clever. They have created a no-win situation for Jesus.

What does Jesus say? Nothing. Instead, he begins to write on the ground with his finger. This is the first and only time recorded that Jesus writes anything. Even though he is not formally trained (as far as we know), he is able to read scriptures, and now we learn he can write. What is he writing?

Maybe what he is writing are the Ten Commandments. These scriptures specifically mention he is using his finger, which could be an allusion to the Ten Commandments inscribed by the "finger of God" (Exodus 31:18). It also may be symbolic in that Jesus has the same authority as God. Other commentaries mention he is using it as a distraction to play for time. Still others conjecture he is writing out the names and various sins of the accusers. This is my favorite theory, although we cannot know. We know one thing from the Bible — he is silent.

The Pharisees and the mob continue to press him to answer, so sure of their foolproof plan, but he keeps on writing in the dust. He knows the heart of every man, and they are unprepared for the Son of God's divine wisdom and righteousness.

> "When they kept questioning him, he straightened up and said to them, "Let any one of you who is without sin be the first to throw a stone at her." Again he stooped down and wrote on the ground." — John 8:7-8

These men might be shocked by what he is writing and what he says, but what makes them leave without one of them throwing a stone? Something supernatural takes place. They are tried, convicted and ashamed. They see their own unworthiness. They are pierced to the heart.

It is not Jesus' intent to condemn them, but to reveal their sins for them to repent. He would have no one die in sin; even those who were trying to trick him and cause his death. He forgives all who repent.

The first ones to leave are the oldest, probably because they know they have the longest list of sins, until there is no one left but Jesus and the woman. John 8:10-11 records the dramatic end of this story:

> "Jesus straightened up and asked her, 'Woman, where are they? Has no one condemned you?' 'No one, sir,' she said. 'Then neither do I condemn you,' Jesus declared. 'Go now and leave your life of sin.'"

Even though I have read this story more than a hundred times, I still can't get over the fact that no one threw a stone at the woman. They have the perfect scheme; this is the evildoers' chance to silence Jesus, and even if Jesus' words have instead convicted them, they could still throw a stone in defiance. This is a mob scene and mobs are unreasonable and uncontrollable, full of bravado and righteousness. Bloodlust overwhelms them when the woman is brought before Jesus. However, he is no ordinary man. He is the Son of God, Jesus the Christ.

The Spirit of God fills the courtyard, causing fear and trembling. No one dares to throw a stone. The fear of God stops them, not merely a sense of guilt or an awareness of their own sin. They are confronted with the power of the presence of God. Not one person remained in the temple — except for this woman and Jesus.

According to the scriptures, this is the first time Jesus looks up at the woman. Until then, he has been writing in the dust. He knows she is there against her will. He knows she is a pawn in the plan to set him up. He knows she is humiliated, helpless, and frightened.

With the Presence of God overwhelming the crowd so everyone leaves, why is she still there? Why does she not run the first chance she gets? She is without hope. She is condemned. She awaits judgment. She prepares for death. She, too, is convicted of her sins.

When he looks up, his eyes fill with compassion. I can imagine she hangs her head in shame, unable to comprehend what has happened, unable to look him in the eyes. She was facing certain death and is now unaccountably free. All the men have fled.

"Woman, where are they? Has no one condemned you?"

He speaks so tenderly. His first words uplift her. They do not add to her humiliation. He does not revile her or call her a whore, sinner, or hussy. He calls her what she is — a woman.

She responds with a minimum of words. "No one, sir."

"Neither do I condemn you. Go now and leave your life of sin."

Jesus is the only one in this entire situation who is truly without sin. He has every right to stone her or at the least verbally condemn her for her sinful life.

Just as the Samaritan woman at the well, Jesus responds without condemnation. These two women are sexually promiscuous, the worst thing a woman can be. Other than a murderer, a woman who is immoral is the worst of sinners.

How does Jesus respond to these women? He responds without condemnation, with perfect grace. He is the holy Son of God. If he were merely a man, he might admonish them to repent, seek forgiveness, go to church and change their lives. However, Jesus says little:

> "Then neither do I condemn you," Jesus declared. "Go now and leave your life of sin." — John 8:11b

This is Christ's "grace freely given" to a woman who is under condemnation by Mosaic Law and who has done nothing to deserve God's forgiveness. She has not repented. She has not had the opportunity to change her life for the better. She has done nothing to merit forgiveness.

In fact, she has not even come to Jesus of her own volition. She did not seek him out. She is brought against her will to him. She does not have a penitent heart — not to begin with. But something changes within her. She experiences something supernatural when the Spirit of God descends, surrounds, and overwhelms the hearts of everyone in the crowd.

Why does Jesus forgive her? He sees her heart; sees what others can't. He knows her whole life; how she got into this situation and who God intended her to be. He sees her fallen state, her pitiable circumstances, her shame, and her desire to be redeemed.

Some ancient manuscripts left this whole story out because of Jesus' response to this adulterous woman. There was some fear among the early church fathers that people would get the idea Jesus condoned sexual immorality, and this woman received forgiveness without having repented. It caused considerable controversy among church leaders because the church was given the power to forgive sins, but through absolution.[26]

Jesus does tell the woman to leave her life of sin. How is she going to do this? This leaves the impression she is a prostitute. If so, she must find another way to make a living.

This is no easy task for a wanton woman, a known prostitute, a woman without resources. She will have to move to a place where no one knows her and hope she can find a man who will marry her and give her a respectable life. Her espoused will no longer want to marry her because of this public humiliation. He would be a laughingstock. She has nothing to live for now. She might as well be dead. Her life is over.

Jesus is telling her to leave her life of sin. In other words, she is to stop what she's been doing and lead a new life. Given her situation, what life could she have? The best life is right before her, standing with his hand out. If you were she, what would you do? Follow Jesus? I would. In fact, I did.

This woman's life is forever changed. She expects condemnation and death and instead receives forgiveness and life eternal. She is not quite a leper, yet she is one of society's castoffs; used, abused, and diminished. Angry, self-righteous men have publicly humiliated her. Not only that but she has been brought into the temple courtyard to face a huge crowd. Whatever she was doing in secret is now revealed to all in the light of day.

This man who is to judge her says nothing, does nothing, and then she feels tremendous power emanating from him. Everyone else leaves. Her accusers are gone. She stands alone before this stranger.

He looks at her and, inexplicably, she sees in his eyes his love for her. It touches the deepest part of her soul. He sees her. No one has ever "seen" her. She is overcome with the knowledge of her own sin, and she repents. In that moment she thinks, if he can love me when I do not deserve it, then I will be his forever. I will follow him no matter what comes. From this day forward, I am his.

~ ~ ~ ~ ~

MEDITATION

We have all done things of which we are not proud.

In fact, some of us may have done something so terrible we cannot even imagine ever being forgiven for it. We will carry around this condemnation and guilt for years, feeling it is the cross we must bear because of our great sin.

Stop. This is wrong. If you have accepted Jesus as Lord and repented, you are forgiven. You are forgiven for not only the terrible sin you bear, but for all your sins, for all time. You only have to accept it. It is freely given. Freely receive it. Lay your sins at the altar of God and leave them there. Do not pick them up again. You are free. In Christ, there is no condemnation. You have not earned or deserved this gift of grace, but it is yours nonetheless.

For it is by grace you have been saved, through faith — and this is not from yourselves, it is the gift of God — not by works, so that no one can boast. — Ephesians 2:8-9

Study Guide Questions

WANTON WOMAN

— List three things you want to remember about the Wanton Woman.

— Where does this woman meet Jesus? Is the location significant?

— What does this story tell you about how Jesus responds to women who are undesirable or are being harshly judged by society?

— What would be your reaction if you were this woman, realizing all of a sudden your accusers are gone? How would this change your life?

— How has this story of the wanton woman freed you from feeling guilt over something you have done?

— Being divorced or single can make a person feel lonely in the church — outside the "circle." What steps can be taken to create greater fellowship opportunities for unmarried members of the congregation? List three possibilities that can be implemented.

NOTES

XV

MARY MAGDALENE

If you have wondered if Jesus loves and respects women, his encounters with Mary Magdalene will surely convince you. There is no dispute that she is the first of his disciples to whom he reveals his resurrected body.

As we study this amazing woman, I want you to be ever mindful of this. There is something transcendent in this fact — a fact no amount of analytical interpretation can remove — Jesus chose her first from among all the rest. The significance of this choice is not something to lord over men but to uphold and validate all Christian women.

Other than her role in the resurrection story, we don't know much about Mary Magdalene through the scriptures, except that she has seven demons cast out of her, is a disciple of Jesus and follows him from Galilee all the way to the tomb — and even beyond. Unlike some among the Twelve, she follows him without wavering. Her presence at the crucifixion and resurrection forces us to recognize her as someone who stands out, as someone who is given honor and importance by the Son of God.

Mary Magdalene is a controversial figure. I caution you that any serious study of this Gospel woman leads to questioning much of what has been written and spoken about her. Her appearance at the end of Jesus' life and the importance he gives her by revealing himself cannot be denied by anyone, but her presence makes many men uncomfortable and confuses many women. For this reason alone, we all need to better understand the significance of Mary Magdalene and her encounter and relationship with Jesus.

Based on recent biblical scholarship and the unearthing of ancient manuscripts, Mary Magdalene's story is finally being told. Her encounter with Jesus as well as their unique relationship brings new revelation to Christian women who may see their role in the church and their evangelism curtailed or diminished by long-held and incorrect assumptions about women, which are now being corrected.

DISCIPLE

Mary Magdalene was an ardent disciple of Jesus. She is not one of the Twelve, but she is one of at least three women whose names are recorded as being Jesus' traveling companions. We first read of her in Luke 8:1-3:

> "After this, Jesus traveled about from one town and village to another, proclaiming the good news of the kingdom of God. The Twelve were with him, and also some women who had been cured of evil spirits and diseases: Mary (called Magdalene) from whom seven demons had come out; Joanna the wife of Chuza, the manager of Herod's household; Susanna; and many others. These women were helping to support them out of their own means."

This passage is extremely revealing. Mary Magdalene is noted as one who is "with" Jesus and the Twelve. She is one of a specific list of women disciples who Luke records. She also provides for Jesus out of her own means throughout his ministry. Where Jesus goes, she goes. When Jesus stays somewhere, she stays. When he travels, she travels. She is with him when he performs miracles, when he teaches, when he is hailed as a king, when he is arrested, and when he is crucified. She is there when he conquers death.

The other thing we learn about her is that her conversion is so dramatic that she is not one of the "women who had been cured of evil spirits and diseases," but "Mary (called Magdalene)... "

She is given a name and a place of origin. Magdala is on the coast of the Sea of Galilee. From excavations completed in the 1970s, it has been ascertained that Magdala (also called Migdal, Magadan and Dalmanthuna) was a fishing village. The historical record also indicates that Magdala was a center for boat building. It had a prosperous economy until AD 66 when it was caught up in the revolt against Rome and all its inhabitants were slaughtered or enslaved.[27]

In addition to her name and place of origin, Luke makes reference to details about her deliverance from evil. Luke only has to say, "You know, the one with seven demons cast out of her," and everyone will affirm, "Of course, Mary from Magdala."

Do you ever wonder why we don't have this dramatic story of Mary's deliverance in the Gospels? We know about the man in the graveyard and his deliverance from "Legion," but of her deliverance, we only know she had seven demons cast out.

Our assumption is that this dramatic exorcism actually occurred. There is no written record of it, so we are left to speculate that it did not happen publicly. It might have happened when she was alone with Jesus. Whatever happened, she is instantly transformed.

Perhaps she sought him out, hearing that the great rabbi Jesus has the power to heal. We know she must have been under great spiritual bondage. We can only speculate as to what is wrong with her. There are some myths suggesting Mary was involved in one of the mystical Jewish cults of those days, making her susceptible to demon possession and receptive to deliverance.

Whatever happened, Mary is transformed from someone to be pitied or feared into a woman of righteousness and importance among the disciples. Her acceptance by the Twelve indicates it is Jesus who brings her into the close-knit group of traveling companions.

He doesn't always do this. After he delivered the man named "Legion" from his demons, Jesus commanded him to stay home. Mary from Magdala is different. She is welcomed into the band of Jesus' closest followers. When Jesus calls Peter, Matthew, John and the rest he says, "Come follow me" and they follow. The same is true of Mary Magdalene. She leaves everything behind to follow him for the rest of her life.

The Gospel of Luke records her name along with Joanna's and Susanna's. She is not merely one of the hangers-on, the curious, or part of the crowd accumulating around Jesus wherever he goes. She is given a specific identification with the Twelve. She is included by name with the women who "support them out of their own means," so we can guess she has an income of some sort. She is a woman who may have owned land and many possessions, but unlike the rich young ruler, she leaves everything behind to follow Jesus.

There is one more thing we can glean from Luke's passage. It begins with "After this." After what? After Jesus raises the Widow of Nain's son from the dead, after he secretly reveals to John the Baptist he is the Messiah, and after a "sinful" woman anoints him. This is one of the reasons many Biblical scholars believe Mary Magdalene is the "sinful" Mary who anoints Jesus' feet before becoming one of his disciples.

But we must pause here and vehemently refute the notion that Mary Magdalene was a prostitute. There is absolutely no evidence in the Gospels. That she is severely afflicted and delivered by Jesus does not mean she is in the flesh trade. This is an unfair and chauvinistic assumption promulgated for centuries and must be corrected. Whether she had seven demons of lust or seven demons of anger, fear, grief, pain, bitterness, occultism and disease cast out is irrelevant; she is freed early on in Jesus' ministry and is with him from then on.

Where does this myth come from? Is it important? Yes, it is important. Would it make a difference to you if every time the church mentions Peter, they said, "Peter, the liar and betrayer of Jesus." Of course it would. Peter repents and is given a great ministry. Mary Magdalene is delivered, restored and is also given a great ministry. Her previous life before Jesus is irrelevant except for the fact her personal encounter with him changes her forever.

The assumption that her life before Jesus is in the sex trade is based solely on the episode of the "sinful woman" who anoints Jesus. How do we leap from that to Mary Magdalene being a prostitute? And how do we ascertain this?

As stated earlier, this notion of Mary being a prostitute originated with Pope Gregory I who speculated in his Homily that Mary of Bethany and Mary Magdalene are one and the same. She is "sinful," has seven demons cast out of her and has access to expensive spikenard used by courtesans; therefore, she must be a prostitute.

Later, in the 12th century, St. Augustine tries to redeem Mary Magdalene's reputation and calls her the "apostle of the apostles." For whatever reason, his view doesn't stick and it isn't until Vatican II (1962-65) that the Catholic Church changes the scripture reading for St. Mary Magdalene's feast day from the redemption of a sinful woman to Mary's encounter with Jesus at the tomb in John 20. But still, the representation of Mary Magdalene as a prostitute persists.

John's Gospel repeats this story and categorically states that the woman who anoints Jesus is Mary of Bethany (the pure, sitting-at-Jesus'-feet-Mary). This should be enough to dispel the myth that Mary Magdalene is the "sinner" and a prostitute.

There is nothing we can do about the fact ancient and modern historians and writers defame such an important female figure, but what we must keep in mind is the indisputable fact that Jesus chose to appear first to this Mary after his resurrection; the one whose heart was pure, whose faith was steadfast, who waited with expectation for him to fulfill his prophecy at the tomb — the "apostle of the apostles" — Mary Magdalene.

FRIEND

> "Now after He had risen early on the first day of the week, He first appeared to Mary Magdalene, from whom He had cast out seven demons." — Mark 16:9

After his resurrection, Jesus speaks to her and asks her to tell others. He trusts her enough to ask her to give his disciples the earth-shattering news — "He is risen!" This speaks of their deep bond, his trust in her, and his complete acceptance of her as a leader. Jesus is not a fool. He knows she will not be believed. Despite this, he believes in her and sends her forth. It is a great honor and an acknowledgment of the capability of her gender to spread the Good News.

There has been a lot of speculation recently about the relationship existing between Jesus and Mary Magdalene because of Dan Brown's *The DaVinci Code* and a resurgence of interest in the woman with whom Jesus appears to have had a special relationship. Aside from some surprising and revelatory scriptures in the Gnostic Gospels, one has to take a leap into fantasy to assume Jesus and Mary Magdalene were lovers. There is absolutely nothing to indicate a sexual relationship between them in the Canonical Gospels.

To even consider such a thing may seem outrageous and sacrilegious to some; but given the fact Jesus was both fully man and fully God, subject to all man's temptations; it is a bit surprising there is nothing in the Gospels about him struggling with the attractions of the many adoring females who must have followed him. In fact, it borders on the implausible.

One of the reasons this seems farfetched may be that as a 30-year-old Jewish male, and firstborn son, it is surprising he is not at least espoused by that time. Was he espoused or married to Mary Magdalene as some speculate? There is no record. It is sheer conjecture. But then we come to this surprising void when it comes to the story of Mary Magdalene. She is given high honor and then disappears from the Bible.

The early church fathers were good at eliminating any reference to Jesus' relationships with women (except the few we are studying in this book). They focused mostly on his divinity. The whole woman issue was too "messy" and incomprehensible. It was hard enough accepting Gentiles into the church, but women! It is much simpler to reassert Jewish and Greek beliefs that women are weak, ignorant and necessary evils.

All that being said, let us put aside the confusion arising from a romantic relationship that existed between Jesus and Mary Magdalene. It is far more plausible to believe that Jesus and Mary were good friends; they shared a unique friendship. There is a special companionship between them. Perhaps it begins in private when Mary is delivered of her demons or develops through his ministry. Having studied the Samaritan Woman, we know Jesus likes to engage in conversation with intelligent women.

By examining the Anointing Woman, we observe Jesus enjoying the attention of women. And we cannot forget the deeply personal friendship he has with sisters Martha and Mary. Using Jesus' own words in referring to the Anointing Woman, "her many sins have been forgiven — as her great love has shown" (Luke 7:47). Mary Magdalene enjoys the same forgiveness.

Mary Magdalene is delivered of great and crushing burdens ("sins") and her gratitude and love are directed toward her redeemer. She loves him, probably more deeply than any other person in her life. She gives up everything to follow him. She has total faith he is the Messiah.

We know this because we see from the crucifixion scriptures that she does not run away. She stays and risks exposure as one of his disciples, even with the threat of jail or death. In Matthew, Mark and John, she is named as one of those women looking on "at a distance."

> "Many women were there, watching from a distance. They had followed Jesus from Galilee to care for his needs. Among them were Mary Magdalene, Mary the mother of James and Joseph, and the mother of Zebedee's sons." — Matthew 27:55, 56

> "There were also some women looking on from a distance, among whom were Mary Magdalene, and Mary the mother of James the Less and Joses, and Salome." — Mark 15:40

> "Near the cross of Jesus stood his mother, his mother's sister, Mary the wife of Clopas, and Mary Magdalene." — John 19:25

The Gospel of John gives us a bird's-eye view of the crucifixion. Whether the women are "in the distance" at first and then approach the foot of the cross, or are there all along, he names them specifically.

Mary, the wife of Clopas, is most likely Jesus' aunt or even possibly his stepsister. According to John who is at the foot of the cross are Jesus's mother, his aunt (or stepsister) and Mary Magdalene.

If ever anyone wants evidence that Mary Magdalene was his wife or espoused, this scripture certainly hints at it. Why is she standing "near the cross" with Jesus' closest female relatives? If she is a former prostitute, "sinner" or even a "groupie," it is doubtful in these tragic circumstances the other Marys would allow her to stand with them. But there is no disagreement. She is accepted.

This close-knit family unit carries on even after they take Jesus down from the cross. These three women stay with the body.

Perhaps they are thinking about his words, which are recorded in John 2:19: "destroy this temple, and in three days I will raise it up;" or in Matthew 16:21:

> "From that time on Jesus began to explain to his disciples that he must go to Jerusalem and suffer many things at the hands of the elders, chief priests, and teachers of the law, and that he must be killed and on the third day be raised to life."

Did Mary Magdalene hear this? Yes. According to this scripture, Jesus explains it to his disciples several times. Is Mary Magdalene one of his disciples? Yes. But is she the only one who really believes what he says? In the midst of this mind-numbing grief and horror, does she have faith he will be raised from the dead?

If she is human, she surely struggled with doubt. But it will be a fleeting doubt. She has great faith. This is one of the reasons she is special to Jesus. She takes in his words and incorporates them into her heart. She has been miraculously healed. She knows the truth deep in her spirit. She has supernatural faith.

> "Mary Magdalene and Mary the mother of Joseph saw where He was laid." — Mark 15:47

> "Mary Magdalene and the other Mary were sitting there opposite the tomb." — Matthew 27:61

When everyone else ran away, hid, or tried to absorb the shock of their Master's demise in whatever way they could (think of Peter who wrestles with his guilt over denying his Master); Mary Magdalene and "the other Mary" (probably Mary of Clopas) stay at the tomb in vigil.

Jesus' mother is now in the care of John and is not in attendance.

As someone who has lost a son in a tragic way, I can completely understand why she gave the burial vigil to someone else. Watching her precious firstborn die a horrible death must have been excruciating, mentally and physically exhausting. That she gives this task over to Mary Magdalene is significant. It is Mary Magdalene and "the other Mary" who remain behind, "sitting opposite the tomb." This indicates a relationship between the Marys.

When reading the Gospel accounts of the resurrection, we can't help but notice differences. Matthew says it is Mary Magdalene and "the other Mary," Mark says it is Mary Magdalene, Mary the mother of James and Salome; John says it is only Mary Magdalene, and Luke, rather reluctantly admits it is Mary Magdalene, Joanna, Mary the mother of James and "others." (Matthew 28:1, Mark 16:1, John 20:1, Luke 24:10)

However, no matter which Gospel account you read, they all agree Mary Magdalene is there at the time Jesus rises from the dead. Those with her are women. At that moment in time when the impossible becomes possible, when Jesus overcomes the power of death; the ones who witness it are Mary Magdalene and the other women. This event is at the crux of the Gospels, the Good News of the New Testament.

Do you feel a rush of pride and honor that during the resurrection, the ones who are there are women? Women may have been silenced, marginalized, and dismissed throughout the Gospels, but at this particular time, their presence is front and center. At this moment, the whole of Christian belief rests on the testimonies of a few women, and then in John's Gospel, Jesus appears to one lone woman — Mary from Magdala.

> "Now after He had risen early on the first day of the week, He first appeared to Mary Magdalene, from whom He had cast out seven demons." — Mark 16:9

APOSTLE/EVANGELIST

There are some Biblical scholars today who, as a result of St. Augustine's view, designate Mary Magdalene as the Apostle of the Apostles. The reason for this elevation of her status is due to John's Gospel account of her unique face-to-face encounter with the risen Christ. Let us look at how John describes it in Chapter 20:11-17:

"Now Mary stood outside the tomb crying. As she wept, she bent over to look into the tomb and saw two angels in white, seated where Jesus' body had been, one at the head and the other at the foot. They asked her, 'Woman, why are you crying?'

'They have taken my Lord away,' she said, 'And I don't know where they have put him.' At this, she turned around and saw Jesus standing there, but she did not realize it was Jesus.

He asked her, 'Woman, why are you crying? Who is it you are looking for?' Thinking he was the gardener, she said, 'Sir, if you have carried him away, tell me where you have put him, and I will get him.'

Jesus said to her, 'Mary.' She turned toward him and cried, '*Rabboni*!'

Jesus said, 'Do not hold onto me, for I have not yet ascended to the Father. Go instead to my brothers and tell them, I am ascending to my Father and your Father; to my God and your God.'"

There is much we can glean from these scriptures, but the most notable statement is verse 17: "Go instead to my brothers and tell them..." The risen Lord's first command is for Mary to find his disciples and give them the news that after three days Jesus has risen from the dead and is physically alive. She becomes the first to declare the Good News.

The other thing I want to note is Jesus calls her by name. "Jesus said to her, 'Mary.'" There is something intimate and loving about the way he says her name so that she suddenly recognizes him and cries out. First, he says, "Woman, why are you crying?" and then he says her name. His first care is for her broken heart. He knows she is grieving, but he also knows her grief will soon turn to gladness when she recognizes him.

Jesus is asking us, "Women, why are you crying?" When we recognize, accept and embrace the truth that Jesus is alive, all our tears will dry and our hearts will soar with joy.

Why didn't Mary recognize him? She is weeping. Her vision is blurred. She sees someone behind her and assumes it must be the gardener. This indicates to a certain extent Mary's belief in the resurrection does not go so far as to incorporate it into the physical. It is one thing to believe in the supernatural power of God, but it is quite another when it enters our ordinary world. We may not immediately recognize it.

Soon after my adult son died, leaving three small children, I went for a walk on the beach, listening to worshipful music, trying somehow to ease my grief. I stayed longer than I should have and got sunburned. I headed back toward the steps leading to the street and saw an older woman standing directly in front of me. She wore white gauzy fabric, a long shirt, and long skirt, her hair curly and white.

As I came near to her I saw her looking right at me. I smiled at her but dropped my eyes. I didn't want her to see my red-rimmed, grief-stricken eyes.

As I passed her she spoke to me, "We must protect the children, don't you agree?" It was such an odd statement. I stopped.

"Excuse me?" I turned and looked closely at her.

"We must protect the children," she said. "Do you see that man?"

I looked where she was pointing. I saw a man playing on the beach with a little girl.

"Do you think there is anything wrong? Do you think he is her father or a stranger?"

Her question startled me and I took another look. Was this an incident of child abduction or molestation? I looked at the scene with critical eyes.

"It's only a father and his daughter," I said.

"It must be," she replied, "but we need to keep watch over the children."

I agreed and took three steps up the stairs, thinking how odd her comments were. I turned back to ask her why she had asked me her question. She was gone. I looked north and south. She was an older woman and I didn't believe she could sprint that fast in either direction. The beach was wide open and there was no way she could disappear, and yet, she was gone.

I knew then I had conversed with an angel. She told me something about the Father's love for his little girl and how it can be misinterpreted through numb, exhausted eyes — as mine were after the loss of my beloved son. It was also a message to stay close to my grandchildren.

But more than that, I realized I had come face-to-face with the supernatural, a supernatural being, an angel. I was not prepared for it. She appeared to be real flesh and blood. The supernatural had entered the natural and I did not comprehend it until she miraculously disappeared.

So I understand why Mary did not see Jesus right away.

I wish more had been written about Mary Magdalene in the Gospels. What eventually happened to her? In the resurrection story she is mentioned at least nine times, then nothing more appears. She should be prominently featured in the Book of Acts, but she is not even mentioned. What do you make of the fact that a powerful woman figure, the one to whom Jesus appeared first after his resurrection, suddenly disappears from the text without explanation?

As women, we have seen these disappearances happen all too frequently, and maybe we have even experienced it personally. The silencing of women and the erasing of women's contributions in history are "legion."

Today, women are given a voice as never before. We are receiving a new revelation from the Holy Spirit. It is no coincidence that in these times, when the church is desperate for laborers in the field, Mary Magdalene's story is resurfacing and she is once again being called the "Apostle of the Apostles."

It is not a coincidence that writings from the first to the fourth centuries, which have only recently been discovered and translated, are giving us a new picture of the church as God intended with no separation: "There is neither Jew nor Gentile, neither slave nor free, nor is there male or female, for you are all one in Christ Jesus" (Galatians 3:28).

All are equal in God's eyes. No law can dictate or supersede God's call. It is not by mere chance Biblical scholars are beginning to excise many centuries of myth and error from patriarchal dogma and begin to permit women to freely answer the call of God.

Because Mary Magdalene is completely missing from the New Testament after the resurrection, she may have had even greater influence in her day than we can possibly know; carrying out the Savior's message of freedom and grace, empowering women as Jesus empowered her.

None of the Gospel writers are entirely comfortable with her, but because the Savior chose to appear first to her after his resurrection; she became the first witness and the first evangelist to deliver the message that Jesus Christ has risen from the dead. This has not changed over millennia.

Her "disappearance" gives further credence to the belief that Mary Magdalene not only went on sharing the teachings of Jesus, but her ministry was powerful and pervasive. This disappearance is too obvious. How can it be the one to whom Jesus announces his resurrection loses all credibility among the other disciples?

Could there have been jealousy among the disciples? "Why did he appear to her and not me?" "Was I not the one he called The Rock?" "Was I not the one he loved best?" "Was I not loyal and faithful?"

It is possible. We have several accounts recorded in the Gospels where the Twelve are seen to jockey for position (Matthew 18:1, 20:20-21; Mark 10:35-37). It is not that hard to believe that once Jesus ascended to heaven, Mary Magdalene was rejected as one of The Way's leaders (The Way was the name given to the early church: Acts 24:14).

The Gospels may have dropped Mary after the resurrection, but there are many outside texts that have been discovered, such as the Gnostic Gospels, that give clues as to what happened to her.

By the time the First Council of Nicaea met for the codification of Christian doctrine (AD 325), Hellenization was pervasive throughout the new Eastern Roman Empire under Emperor Diocletian (AD 284-305) and Emperor Constantine (AD 306-337).

Hellenization is a term that describes the extensive influence of ancient Greek culture, philosophy, and language on countries conquered by Alexander the Great (356-323 BC). Centuries later, the Romans, particularly the emperors, revered Alexander's achievements and adopted Greek ideas, becoming "Hellenized".

In Jesus' day, under Roman rule, the Hellenization of Palestine was of grave concern to the Jewish leaders. The influence of Greco-Roman culture on Jewish life was extremely disruptive, resulting in a split between the more wealthy and liberal Sadducees, who welcomed and practiced Greek ways, and the ultra-conservative Pharisees, who aggressively tried to maintain Jewish identity by a rigid adherence to Mosaic Law.

We see this rift throughout the Gospels. In addition, Saul of Tarsus, who takes the Greek name Paul, is also influenced by Hellenization. Many Jewish Christians took Greek names.

While Hellenization brought forth wonderful views on democracy, art and literature, it also brought the Greek belief that women were little better than slaves, unable to be educated, and necessary only for childbearing.[28]

This view was regrettably retained by the First Council of Nicaea as the Christian bishops and religious leaders worked to remove heresy from Christian doctrine. Any indication that Jesus considered his women followers equal to the Twelve would never be accepted by the early church fathers. Further, any writings that gave Mary Magdalene power or authority in the church would have been suppressed.

Fortunately for women, the resurrected Jesus in his infinite wisdom appeared to Mary Magdalene first and commanded her to tell his disciples, so there is little any council, canon or church can do to change this fact in the Gospels. The best they can do is undermine Mary's importance by calling her a prostitute, the lowest of the lows, a sinner, a woman possessed of seven demons.

Under the rule of the "Christian" Roman emperor Constantine, additional writings about Jesus were deemed heretical. A concerted effort was made to define orthodox Christianity by having all other scriptural variations destroyed. It has recently come to light that early Christians hid additional writings deep in the recesses of caves. These are known as the Gnostic Gospels (from the Greek word *gnosis*, meaning "spiritual knowledge") and continue to be extremely controversial in the church.

These writings are thought to have originated between the first or early second centuries AD[29] (the same period as the Canonical Gospels), but because they deal with transcendental issues, such as what Jesus said after his resurrection and more about Mary Magdalene and her prominence among the Apostles, they were considered heretical by the Council of Nicaea.

The Berlin Gnostic Codex from the early fourth or fifth century AD (including the Gospel of Mary; The Sophia [wisdom] of Jesus Christ and the Acts of Peter, among others) was discovered in Cairo, Egypt and purchased by German scholar Dr. Carl Reinhardt who brought it to Berlin in 1896. These Gnostic Gospels only became available to the public in the 1970s.[30]

The Oxyrhynchus papyri, dating from the first through sixth centuries AD, were discovered in 1896 in a rubbish dump in Egypt. They include thousands of Latin and Greek literary and theological writings. There are also sections of the Old and New Testament.

The Gnostic Gospels corroborated these previous discoveries, including the Gospels of Mary, Thomas, Peter and James.[31]

The extensive Nag Hammadi library (includes thirteen papyrus books: the Gospel of Thomas, the Gospel of Phillip, the Gospel of Truth, and numerous other documents; possibly written in AD 120-150) was discovered in 1945 in Upper Egypt. After decades of painstaking translation, these writings were published in the 1970s.[32]

It should be noted that the Gnostic Gospels, and other ancient writings discovered along with them, are not recognized by most Christian denominations as authoritative scripture, and I am not advocating them as such.

For the serious Bible student, it is important to understand how scripture was canonized. The reason for the "woman gap" may be explained by the loss of many writings over the millennia (parts of the Berlin Gnostic Codex were used as fire kindling before their importance came to light). As a Christian woman who has often wondered about Mary Magdalene and her ministry, I gratefully welcome these writings in spite of my conditioning to dismiss them as "unscriptural."

In the Gospel of Thomas, one of the Gnostic Gospels, there are important passages about Mary Magdalene indicating she is ostracized by some of the disciples after Jesus' ascension.

In Section 114, Peter says, "Let Mary leave us, for women are not worthy of the Life." Peter's hostility toward Mary is also recorded in the Gospel of Mary which indicates Peter is jealous and threatened by Mary's leadership and influence, even as Levi (Matthew) defends her, saying "she was loved most of all."[33]

It's not hard to imagine without Jesus in their midst, this rough Galilean's pride and chauvinism resurfaces and Mary hasn't got a chance. We want to believe the best of Peter, but even the Apostle Paul had a run-in with Peter about the inclusion of Gentiles by The Way.

Peter was the recognized authority of the First Church. Peter was a man of great passion, persuasion and stature. I love Peter because he is so roughly human; he made terrible mistakes, but he loved Jesus, believed in him, started the first church, and took Jesus' message to the world.

His culture, upbringing, and personal disposition may have led him to cut Mary Magdalene out of the church leadership, which is unfortunate but understandable. He was a big personality. She was a big personality. He was not one to share his "mandate" to be the "Rock" of the church. Under constant threat of persecution, the fledgling church needed unity. I believe Mary understood this and departed Jerusalem of her own volition, leaving the church in Peter's capable hands.

One widely held belief is that Mary leaves Jerusalem soon after Jesus' ascension and travels with Jesus' mother and the Apostle John to Ephesus in Turkey. There is further speculation that she even helps John write his Gospel. (Is this perhaps why the story of the Samaritan woman is only recorded in John?) After the death of Jesus' mother, Mary Magdalene books passage on a ship going north and ends up in France where she lives out her days.

One legend has it that she is such a dynamic force after the ascension, she travels to Rome and shares Christianity's Good News with Tiberius

Caesar, and is responsible for getting Pontius Pilate removed from office.

Another legend and long-held belief is that fourteen years after the ascension, Mary [Magdalene], Martha, Lazarus, Mary Jacobe, Maximin, Salome, Cedonius (the blind man who had received his sight), Marcella and Sara (handmaidens) are set adrift by the Jews without a rudder, paddles, or sails. Through miraculous intervention, guided by an angel, their boat lands safely on the southern coast of France where they receive a warm welcome.

Mary Magdalene and her companions preach the gospel and the whole village of Provence becomes believers. Lazarus becomes the first bishop of Marseille and Maximin becomes Bishop of Aix. Mary retreats to a grotto and lives out her final days in contemplation and prayer.

Today her bones (including her skull) are in fact in a golden reliquary in a crypt in the Basilica to Mary Magdalene in Saint Maximin de Provence, France where she is held in high regard.[34]

The most widely held belief is Mary Magdalene leaves Jerusalem and travels to southern France, to a place called La Sainte Baume where she lives for another thirty years. She has an extraordinary healing ministry and is the first to bring the message of salvation to the pagans of Europe.

There is a persistent and even wilder belief, promoted by Dan Brown in his 2003 bestseller, *The DaVinci Code*, that Mary Magdalene was Jesus' wife and the mother of a daughter, who started the Merovingian line of the first kings of France.[35]

Unfortunately, we cannot know if any of these things are factual. They are lost to us in the annals of time. There are many myths and legends about Mary, ranging from the plausible to the fantastic. We know for sure Mary Magdalene made an indelible impact on Jesus, and she continues to make an impact on Christian women.

As women, we must not let Mary Magdalene's importance diminish. Even without the Gnostic Gospels, we have enough information about her to assert she was certainly not a prostitute, but more likely an "Apostle to the Apostles," and her ministry began when Jesus said to her, "go tell my disciples... "

Jesus' command to her is his command to us. "Go and tell." Speak the words of truth about the Good News — Jesus has risen, he loves and honors women, and he sets us free to be blessings and to influence the world. He did not tell us to be quiet. Through Mary Magdalene, he gave us permission to speak.

She will not be denied. Her power is our power. Her voice is our voice.

~ ~ ~ ~ ~

MEDITATION

Understanding Mary Magdalene and how she fits into the Gospels and the life of Jesus can become troubling because of all the controversy that has always surrounded her. Let us put all that aside and meditate on her as a woman we can emulate. She was faithful to the end. She was devout, compassionate, and grateful. She gave of her finances and offered all she had. She was intelligent, loving, and mysterious.

Imagine yourself as Mary Magdalene. Meditate on her devotion, her sacrifice, and her faith. Jesus loved her as He loves you. Accept God's love for you and give him everything you have.

Dear friends, let us love one another, for love comes from God. Everyone who loves has been born of God and knows God.
— 1 John 4:7

Study Guide Questions

MARY MAGDALENE

— List three things you want to remember about Mary Magdalene.

— In what way does Jesus' relationship with Mary Magdalene enhance the power and importance of women?

— By witnessing the culmination of God's plan for mankind's redemption, Mary Magdalene is given a full understanding of Jesus' mission. She is singled out by Jesus and becomes the "Apostle of the Apostles." Discuss what this means to women in general and you specifically.

— Does Mary Magdalene's story empower you? How? Because of her, do you think women can be given divine assignments, powerful ministries, and leadership opportunities?

— What do you think happened to Mary Magdalene? Why is she not mentioned again after the Gospels?

— What can you do to bring Mary Magdalene's story to the church and reveal her true character and importance? Discuss two possibilities.

NOTES

XVI

WOMEN DISCIPLES

Did you know Jesus had many women disciples? Because of the way the Gospels are written and the times in which they were written, most of us don't realize how many women disciples walked with Jesus; women who are equally as visible as the Twelve. They are visible and yet invisible

During the first century, women were rarely recognized for their contributions and spirituality. They were no seen as equals, but a step above slaves who were incapable of learning, teaching or leading. As hard as it is to believe, this gender bias continues to influence the church two thousand years later.

It is enough to make a Christian woman cry out with frustration — if not for the actions and words of Jesus, the Son of God. He deliberately disregarded gender in those days. By understanding how he interacted with and elevated women, Christian women are able to overcome the bias that can keep them from fulfilling their God-given calling.

Thank you, Jesus, for setting women free.

These women disciples walk beside him. They eat with him. They talk with him. They listen and absorb every word he says. They ask him questions and he answers. They discuss his words with the other disciples. They prepare meals, wash clothes, mend sandals, tend wounds, secure lodging, buy or gather food, comfort the broken-hearted, and evangelize.

Most importantly, they commit their lives to Jesus and to the establishment of the Kingdom of God on Earth. In those times, this circumstance is most unusual. Jewish women are not educated as they are today. They are not allowed to study with a rabbi. They certainly do not travel with a band of men from town to town, unless they are wanton women. Jesus made it clear in his ministry he accepts women as well as men.

If you are not convinced, re-read the chapter on Martha and Mary. Who chose most wisely, the woman doing traditional female tasks or her sister who is breaking the gender rules, sitting at Jesus' feet? From the beginning of his ministry, women are in attendance. In addition, they are noticeably with him at the end — and beyond. Women who follow Jesus are his disciples.

You might be as surprised as I am to find that from among the many anonymous women who walk with Jesus and care for his and the apostles' needs, several women are identified by name. In Luke 8:1-3, we learn about some of them:

> "After this, Jesus travelled about from one town and village to another, proclaiming the good news of the kingdom of God.

> "The Twelve were with him, and also some women who had been cured of evil spirits and diseases: Mary (called Magdalene) from whom seven demons had come out; Joanna the wife of Chuza, the manager of Herod's household; Susanna; and many others. These women were helping to support them out of their own means."

I am so thankful for this scripture. It gives us a glimpse into the day-to-day activity of the women disciples. These women are specifically mentioned in all the Gospels as being at Jesus' crucifixion. Out of the "many" the scriptures refer to, these women's names are used. They have risen from the unidentified and are recognized by all four Gospel writers. This is probably because their names are known in the early church when the Gospels are written.

More important to us as women, when you read the following scriptures, you get a sense that although the apostles have fled (except for Apostle John), "many women" remain to witness the terrible torture and death of Jesus. These are dedicated, fully committed disciples. All the Gospel writers feel compelled to mention their presence.

> "Many women were there, watching from a distance. They had followed Jesus from Galilee to care for his needs. Among them were Mary Magdalene, Mary the mother of James and Joseph, and the mother of Zebedee's sons." — Matthew 27:55-56

> "Some women were watching from a distance. Among them was Mary Magdalene, Mary the mother of James the younger and of Joseph, and Salome. In Galilee these women had followed him and cared for his needs. Many other women who had come up with him to Jerusalem were also there." — Mark 15:40-41

> "When all the people who had gathered to witness this sight saw what took place, they beat their breasts and went away. But all those who knew him, including the women who had followed him from Galilee, stood at a distance, watching these things." — Luke 23:48-49

> "Near the cross of Jesus stood his mother, his mother's

sister, Mary the wife of Clopas, and Mary Magdalene." — John 19:25

"The women who had come with Jesus from Galilee followed Joseph and saw the tomb and how his body was laid in it." — Luke 23:55

"It was Mary Magdalene, Joanna, Mary the mother of James, and the others with them who told this [that the tomb was empty] to the apostles. But they did not believe the women because their words seemed to them like nonsense." — Luke 24:10-11

Reading these scriptures from each of the Gospels is inspiring, even while contemplating the terrible price Jesus paid for our sins. There, at the cross, are these women who love Jesus, who care for him and who follow Him to the end. These are not hangers-on or the curious. This is a crowd of women whose lives have been forever changed by Jesus.

Three of the Gospels indicate that many of these women have been with Jesus since he came from Galilee, which is where he first called his twelve disciples. Many women are "called" at the same time. Although they are not named, they still make an impact on those around them.

It is probable these women disciples are among the seventy-two disciples mentioned in Luke 10:1 whom Jesus sends out to heal the sick, cast out demons and bring the kingdom of God. He sends them out two-by-two.[36] Does he send them out in this way so both men and women might be prayed for, ministered to and baptized? It is an excellent model for the church today. Both women and men are called upon to evangelize and both genders need to be equipped to go into the field for the harvest.

When the faithful return from their first evangelical mission, the men and women are filled with joy and excitement. Read Luke 10:17-24 to get the full sense of what it is like to be sent by Jesus equipped by the

Holy Spirit. This is truly remarkable. What Jesus says to them when they return should warm the heart. He is saying this to you.

> "The seventy-two returned with joy... 'I have given you authority to trample on snakes and scorpions and to overcome all the power of the enemy; nothing will harm you. However, do not rejoice that the spirits submit to you, but rejoice that your names are written in heaven.'
>
> At that time Jesus, full of joy through the Holy Spirit, said, 'I praise you, Father, Lord of heaven and earth, because you have hidden these things from the wise and learned, and revealed them to little children. Yes, Father, for this is what you were pleased to do. All things have been committed to me by my Father...'
>
> Then he turned to his disciples and said privately, 'Blessed are the eyes that see what you see. For I tell you that many prophets and kings wanted to see what you see but did not see it, and to hear what you hear but did not hear it.'"

I am struck with the fact that when these seventy-two disciples return, their stories fill Jesus with joy. This is one of his best days, certainly. You can imagine them all talking at once as they return, two-by-two. Can you see our Lord's face, grinning from ear to ear, as he nods with understanding and pride in his "little children."

I want you to note that his prayer to the Father in verse 21 does not have him saying, "sons and brothers." No, he says "little children" (i.e. both male and female).

Add to this what we already know in Luke 8:1-3 about the women who followed him, and it is not a great stretch to imagine that many of the seventy-two disciples are women. These women are most certainly among the apostles and other disciples who met in the upper room at Pentecost:

> "They all joined together constantly in prayer, along with the women and Mary the mother of Jesus, and with his brothers." — Acts 1:14

Verse 15 states the number of people in the upper room is one hundred and twenty. If conservatively we estimate a third of them are women, then at least forty women are there and receive the Holy Spirit to become leaders in the newly formed church.

In Luke 23:55, we gain further insight. The women "who had come from Galilee" follow Joseph of Arimathea to the tomb where they put Jesus' body. They do not leave his side for a moment (except when he is under arrest). These same women are more than likely the ones who come with spices to anoint the body for burial and find an empty tomb. We know Mary Magdalene is one of them, so Joanna and Susanna are probably also with her since they are mentioned together.

We also learn from the scant references that many of these women have money of their own. Through their "own means" they care for Jesus and his band of disciples (Luke 8:3). Jesus' messages will penetrate the heart of any woman, but for a well-to-do woman who has everything except respect it will mean everything.

The sweet perfume of God's grace and acceptance makes Jesus highly attractive, and many will follow. Women who are physically, emotionally or spiritually desperate — especially those who have the wherewithal to afford physicians but have exhausted every possibility for healing — will let nothing stand in their way to be touched by this controversial figure Jesus who is said to have the power to heal.

We see this in the story of the "bleeding woman" who breaks all societal barriers to touch the hem of his garment. Do you think she became one of Jesus' disciples after her miraculous healing?

Legal documents from the first century have been discovered which reveal some marriage contracts actually set aside the bride price for the woman's use should her spouse die or divorce her. Other records show land and household expenses were put aside for women. Wills have been recovered which indicate women also inherited "resources." [37] Of course, this information is based on a few surviving documents from the upper classes. Women in the lower classes did not have the same kind of protection, and usually did not leave property records.

Because the Gospels mention these women have their "own means," it is safe to assume they are women of influence, who can dispose of their wealth as they wish. However, I can also imagine there are many more women who are dependent on a father, brothers, sons, or husband who will not allow them to support Jesus.

It must have caused many a family rift, disinheritance, or disavowal of their existence. The price these women pay to follow Jesus is not negligible. There are women who have money and who provided for them out of their own resources and then there are women who left everything to follow Jesus.

JOANNA

We know from Luke 8:1-3 that Joanna is the wife of Chuza, the steward of Herod and she has an encounter with Jesus that changes her life. We know she is his disciple and provides for his needs through her own considerable resources. She is probably aware of his arrest and is one of the many women at his crucifixion. She is mentioned as being with Mary Magdalene at the empty tomb. Her husband, Chuza, is the steward of Herod Antipas who is king of the Jews.[38]

As steward, Chuza is likely to be in charge of Herod's treasury. He will be a man of considerable power, high up in the court. King Herod is tetrarch of Galilee and Perea and has a role in both John the Baptist and Jesus' executions. His father was Herod the Great, the one who tried to kill the baby Jesus by exterminating all the male children under the age of two. The rule of King Herod is powerful and deadly.

Chuza is a Jew in a high position. Some scholars speculate that the title of steward can also mean he is a governor of a certain province, or "chief of house." His office can be compared to Joseph's position in the house of Potiphar — meaning he spoke for the "head" and was the right-hand man.[38]

As the wife of Chuza, Joanna also enjoys a high position at Herod's court and she probably lives a luxurious lifestyle compared to many of the common folk and "sinners" with whom Jesus usually associated. She has everything she needs. Why would she support a penniless and controversial rabbi?

Joanna is one of the women who supported Jesus and his disciples "out of their own means." It is possible she provides a substantial amount into the common coffer and is one of Jesus' biggest funders. Her husband has to be aware of her activities and that she is contributing money to this Jewish prophet who is causing such a stir in the realm. That he doesn't stop her must mean he either doesn't know what she is doing or he knows and approves.

If he did know, there is something about his wife's encounter with Jesus that changes his mind about Jesus and makes him acquiesce to his wife's devotion. He may actually be a disciple.

Given the context of the verse that mentions Joanna, we can assume she is either now freed of demonic possession or oppression or healed of some life-threatening illness — something that makes Chuza accept Jesus as a great holy man at the least or the promised Messiah at the most, probably due to the miraculous event that made his wife an ardent follower.

It is hard to believe a high-ranking official in Herod's court such as Chuza supports the work of Jesus of Nazareth, but we know from the detailed account of Jesus' trial in the courts of Herod and by Pilate that there were people "in the know" who saw what happened. There are eyewitnesses to Jesus' debasement and torture at the hands of Herod. These accounts do not come from his twelve disciples. Those men ran away when Jesus was arrested.

Although we have no name associated with it, the account of Jesus' trial came from someone. It could be Joanna, Chuza, or an unnamed believer who is in the position to witness what transpired. This might have been the believer and prophet, Manaen, who is known as "a foster brother" or "close companion" of Herod. His small mention in Acts reveals people inside the court of Herod witness the trial and become followers of Jesus:

> "Now in the church at Antioch there were prophets and teachers: Barnabas, Simeon called Niger, Lucius of Cyrene, Manaen (who had been brought up with Herod the tetrarch) and Saul." — Acts 13:1

Regardless of who witnesses the terrible events, we know that Jesus has friends in Herod's court, and not only friends, but believers — and Joanna is one of them. It is important to also mention that many scholars believe that Junia, whom the Bible mentions in Romans 16:7 is Greek for Joanna, and that Joanna is instrumental in the founding of the Church.[39]

> "Greet Andronicus and Junia, my fellow Jews who have been in prison with me. They are outstanding among the apostles, and they were in Christ before I was." — Romans 16:7

Please note Paul states that Junia/Joanna is "outstanding among the apostles." This is important as it indicates women were known as apostles in the founding of the church.

We can only speculate what happens to Chuza, but perhaps like Joanna, he takes the Greek name Andronicus. All this is speculation, but it is not difficult to imagine that with Chuza and Joanna's position in Herod's court, their conversion to The Way will have a big impact.

The atmosphere in Herod's court must have been electrifying, dangerous, and terrifying after the resurrection of Jesus. If you were a believer in Herod's court, what would you do when you heard the news that Jesus was seen alive and walking around?

In AD 36, a few years after the resurrection, Herod Antipas is at war and suffers a great defeat. Soon after, his wife's brother, Agrippa, deposes Herod by order of Agrippa's close friend, the new Roman emperor, Caligula. Declaring himself the "one Lord, one King," in AD 40, Caligula orders his statue to be erected in the Temple of Jerusalem. Civil war is imminent until Agrippa persuades Caligula to rescind this order. These are volatile times. Caligula despises the Jews; the Jews despise the Christians, and the Christians suffer at the hands of both.

It is not hard to believe that in the days following Jesus' death, Joanna and Chuza leave Herod's court, change their names, and become important church leaders. But think about what Joanna gave up to follow Jesus.

SUSANNA

Susanna is only mentioned as being with Joanna and Mary Magdalene as one who uses her own money to support Jesus' ministry (Luke 8:1-3). We can assume she also has independent financial resources. There is not much more we can learn about Susanna except she has an encounter with Jesus and is miraculously healed, either physically or spiritually. The miracle she experiences makes her a disciple of Jesus, which causes her to support him.

Because she is mentioned with these other two women, Mary Magdalene and Joanna, we can surmise Susanna has some special recognition in the early church. She is identified because she is someone people will remember, possibly because she is wealthy, but more likely because she is an evangelist with the story of her miracle to tell. She is probably one of the seventy-two disciples, most likely at the cross, and probably in the upper room at Pentecost. She is also known as a myrrh-bearer, one of the women who brought spices to the tomb.

We don't know much about Susanna but we have learned she contributes to and supports the work of Christ, serving as a model for women. The Christian church today still needs the support of women, both financially and spiritually. It is enriched by their stories of God's power in their lives.

MARY OF CLOPAS

There is so little known about Mary of Clopas that we are left to speculate on who she was. We know she is with Mary Magdalene when Mary goes to the tomb to anoint Jesus' body with myrrh and other burial spices. We know she is one of three "Marys" associated with Jesus, which makes it difficult to identify her. She could be either the daughter or the wife of someone named Clopas (Chlopas or Cleopas), however most scholars agree that she is his wife and not his daughter.

According to Richard Bauckham, professor of New Testament Studies and Bishop Wardlaw Professor at the University of St. Andrews, Scotland, in his excellent book, *Gospel Women: Studies of the Named Women in the Gospels*, there is considerable evidence to assert that Mary of Clopas is the sister-in-law of Mary the mother of Jesus. In other words, she would be Joseph's brother's wife.

She is also Mary, the mother of James the Younger and Joses (or Joseph) who are Jesus' cousins. Or, as indicated in John 19:25, she may be the Virgin Mary's blood sister. There is no actual word in Hebrew or Aramaic for sister-in-law; she is thought to be either a sister (sister-in-law) or cousin.[40] Most scholars do agree that Mary of Clopas is one of Jesus' inner circle, probably a relative, who is present at his execution and his burial.

Some scholars assert Clopas is a variant spelling of Cleopas. If this is true, he may be the one spoken of as the man walking on the road to Emmaus with a "companion" when Jesus appears after his resurrection and walks with them (Luke 24:18). The companion may be his wife, Mary. When you read the scriptures it is equally plausible, in fact more so, that Cleopas is discussing the past events with his wife — someone he can trust — someone who has been there from the beginning.

Luke 24:13-18 and 30 give us the story:

> "Now that same day two of them were going to a village called Emmaus, about seven miles from Jerusalem. They were talking with each other about everything that had happened.
>
> As they talked and discussed these things with each other, Jesus himself came up and walked along with them; but they were kept from recognizing him.
>
> He asked them, 'What are you discussing together as you walk along?' They stood still, their faces downcast. One of them, named Cleopas, asked him, 'Are you the only one visiting Jerusalem who does not know the things that have happened there in these days?'
>
> When he was at the table with them, he took bread, gave thanks, broke it and began to give it to them. Then their eyes were opened and they recognized him, and he disappeared from their sight."

One of the "two" may well be Mary of Clopas, walking with her husband. This encounter occurs right after everyone discovers the empty tomb. Other scholars assert the "companion" is either Luke or Emmaus, a disciple. We don't really know. We only know from the scriptures a man named Cleopas is walking with someone (Luke, Emmaus or Mary of Clopas) when Jesus appears and walks along with them.

I like to envision Mary and Cleopas walking together, discussing what has happened to their beloved Master. Jesus reveals that he is truly the Messiah, the Son of God, who has conquered the grave.

Like other eyewitnesses to Jesus' resurrection, Mary and Cleopas are instantly convinced of his divinity, his power, and his righteousness and they become powerful evangelists. They are likely to be in the upper room at Pentecost, close to the other disciples and founders of the Church; a powerful couple among the young believers, particularly those three thousand people who accept the "Good News" the day Peter speaks under the power of the Holy Spirit in Acts 2:41-47:

> "Those who accepted his message were baptized, and about three thousand were added to their number that day. They devoted themselves to the apostles' teaching and to fellowship, to the breaking of bread and to prayer. Everyone was filled with awe at the many wonders and signs performed by the apostles.
>
> All the believers were together and had everything in common. They sold property and possessions to give to anyone who had need. Every day they continued to meet together in the temple courts. They broke bread in their homes and ate together with glad and sincere hearts, praising God and enjoying the favor of all the people. And the Lord added to their number daily those who were being saved."

SALOME

Salome's name is mentioned two times in the New Testament and is implied in a third scripture. She is one of the women identified at the crucifixion. (This is not the Salome who dances for King Herod and asks for John the Baptist's head.) We don't know much more about her, but the fact Mark writes of her by name indicates she is someone of importance, a woman of prominence in Jesus' circle and a devoted disciple who is there at his death. She is also among the women who "cared for his needs" so she has resources of her own that she uses to support Jesus' ministry.

> "Some women were watching [the crucifixion] from a distance. Among them was Mary Magdalene, Mary the mother of James the younger and of Joseph, and Salome. In Galilee these women had followed him and cared for his needs." — Mark 15:40

> "When the Sabbath was over, Mary Magdalene, Mary the mother of James, and Salome bought spices so that they might go to anoint Jesus's body." — Mark 16:1

> "Many women were there [at the crucifixion], watching from a distance. They had followed Jesus from Galilee to care for his needs. Among them were Mary Magdalene, Mary the mother of James and Joseph, and the mother of Zebedee's sons." — Matthew 27:55-56

The Gospel of Matthew does not mention Salome, but in the context of Mark's account, Salome is probably the mother of Zebedee's sons, Apostles James and John (See Matthew 4:21).

From this scripture, we can surmise that when Salome's sons leave their fishing business to follow Jesus, she follows them. It's a bit odd, but not implausible that a Jewish mother will follow her sons to care for them. We don't know when she joins the band of Jesus' followers. Is it when James and John leave, or later when she realizes her sons are not going to give up their devotion to Jesus?

The scriptures state their mother (also known as Mary Salome) is among the women who join them in Galilee. She is with them from the beginning and is there at the end. There is another reference to the mother of James and John (possibly Mary Salome) in Matthew 20:20-21:

> "Then the mother of Zebedee's sons came to Jesus with her sons and, kneeling down, asked a favor of him. 'What is it you want?' he asked. She said, 'Grant that one of these two sons of mine may sit at your right and the other at your left in your kingdom.'"

We know from the rest of this chapter that her request causes a furor among the other disciples. All of a sudden everyone is jockeying for power and Jesus shakes his head.

"You don't know what you're asking," he replies, telling them that whoever wants to become great must become a servant and whoever wants to be first must become a slave. It's a profound moment, and one that is precipitated by a woman — a mother trying to get the best position for her sons.

If Salome is the mother of Zebedee's sons, then her conversation with Jesus in Matthew 20 indicates a certain relationship exists between them. She comes to petition him. She wants a favor. She feels comfortable asking him. She has access to him. He knows her. She has been with him since the beginning of his ministry in Galilee. She is the mother of two of his chosen Twelve. We don't know how close their relationship is, but they are clearly well acquainted.

According to scripture, she approaches Jesus with James and John beside her. Do you find this odd? What makes James and John come along with their mother to ask this favor of Jesus? As two of the Twelve, they have intimate access to Jesus. They can ask him questions at any time. They have ample opportunity to find him alone and ask to be at his right and at his left in his kingdom. Is there something about the request that makes them uncomfortable? Do they know in their hearts it is the wrong kind of question to ask Jesus?

That leaves Salome. Is she encouraging her sons to secure favorable positions with the great rabbi and prophet? Since she travels with them, I assume she is doing all the motherly things like cooking for them, mending and washing their clothes, and keeping a lookout for an advantage for them.

According to the Gospel of Matthew, this interaction occurs right before Jesus enters Jerusalem and is hailed as king. Everyone in Jesus' entourage knows they are going to Jerusalem. There may be those on hand who believe Jesus will enter Jerusalem, call down fire like Elijah and declare his right to the throne of David. It is no wonder Salome takes this opportunity to secure a position for her sons.

We also see in the scriptures she kneels at Jesus' feet. This may be because she doesn't have daily contact with him or is trying to curry his favor. She shows Jesus great reverence and obeisance — like one gives a king. This seems to indicate she isn't merely traveling with him because of her sons, but because she believes he is a great holy man or even the Messiah. As the mother of two of the apostles, she must hear about all the miraculous things Jesus says and does.

There is something endearing about how brave (or brazen) she is to ask for favor for her sons. This is what mothers do. She is the mother of sons, but she is also Salome. In her heart of hearts, she believes Jesus has come to free them from Roman domination and when He comes into his kingdom, He will need advisers. Her sons fit the bill. I can imagine her at the campfire with her sons James and John, trying to persuade them:

"Say something to him. How will he know if you don't speak up for yourselves? Tomorrow might be too late."

"Aw, mom, you don't understand. Peter's his right-hand man."

"You boys are so much better than Peter. You can't be shy. Tomorrow I'm going to Jesus and ask. There's no harm in asking. And you're coming with me!"

"Aw, mom, do we have to?"

I hope you are laughing because mothers often embarrass their children in their effort to promote and position them. It would be laughable if the truth were not so grim. She didn't know what she was asking. Her sons didn't know. How could they? Jesus will pay the ultimate price to come into his kingdom.

The mother of Zebedee's sons travels three years with the young rabbi from Galilee. With her own eyes she witnesses many miracles — the blind receive their sight, the lame walk, the lepers are free of their disease; her companion, Mary Magdalene, has seven demons cast out of her, a mere five loaves and two fish feed five thousand people, the dead rise from the grave with their burial clothes still wrapped around them.

She has heard Jesus' words about the kingdom of God, the love of God, how the meek will inherit the earth, that he is the way, truth and light and no one comes to God [Yahweh] but through him, and if anyone wants to follow him, she must take up her own cross daily. At Jesus' crucifixion, all these things run through her mind as she sees the brutal end of her greatest hope.

Darkness is on the face of the Earth. Darkness fills Salome's heart and the hearts of Jesus' disciples who do not understand the mysterious ways of God. They do not understand Jesus had to die and rise from death, before being seated at the right hand of God. They could not know this.

It is beyond human understanding. This is why the picture of the cross is so profound — it is the death of everything we believe in and yet conveys the promise of redemption, not because of anything we have done to deserve it, but only by the grace of God.

There are many who believe Salome is actually the sister of Jesus but she comes from Joseph's line, not Mary's. This assertion stems from the belief that Mary is a virgin to the day she dies.

Salome is a stepsister based on the assumption Mary's husband Joseph is a widower with children when they marry. James the brother of Jesus and Salome are Joseph's children from a previous marriage. That's one theory. Another is that Salome is Mary's sister and Jesus' aunt.

The most important thing to remember about Salome, regardless of to whom she is related, is she is with Jesus in Galilee from the beginning, travels with him during his ministry and is among the observers at his crucifixion.

She is one of three women who come to the empty tomb and witness first-hand that Jesus' body is no longer there. I have no doubt she is also one of the disciples in the upper room at Pentecost. She is a named disciple because she has full knowledge of the life and death of Jesus, is transformed by his resurrected presence and has a voice in the early Christian church.

A DISCIPLE OF JESUS

What makes a disciple? A disciple is a student of Jesus. The role of a disciple is to imitate Christ and to fulfill his Great Commission:

> "Therefore go and make disciples of all nations, baptizing them in the name of the Father and of the Son and of the Holy Spirit, and teaching them to obey everything I have commanded you. And surely I am with you always, to the very end of the age." — Matthew 28:19-20

Jesus clearly had more than twelve disciples. In Luke 10: 1,17, Jesus sends out seventy-two disciples. Luke 6:17 says, "He [Jesus] went down with them and stood on a level place. A large crowd of his disciples was there..."

Twelve is not a crowd and seventy-two is not a large group. Through the Gospels we learn that disciples follow Jesus from the moment he calls them until the end and then beyond, as they respond to the risen Savior's

Great Commission (Matthew 28:19), "Go therefore and make disciples of all nations…"

AFTER PENTECOST

As the Church grew, more and more disciples distinguish themselves, and there are a number of women whose names are recorded for all time. I think it is important we know who they are and use this knowledge to encourage us as women to step out into ministry and answer God's call for our lives.

> "In Joppa there was a disciple named Tabitha (which, when translated from the Greek, is Dorcas), who was always doing good and helping the poor." She is particularly noted because Peter raises her from the dead (Acts 9:36-43).

In Acts 12 we learn two more names of women disciples: Mary the mother of Mark and a servant girl named Rhoda. When an angel breaks Peter out of prison, he goes to the nearest church. It is Mark's mother, Mary, who owns the house where believers congregate; in other words, she has established a church in Jerusalem. The young servant Rhoda is also a believer and is so excited that Peter is at the door, she forgets to let him in.

In Acts 16, we first read about Timothy, Paul's protégé, and learn his mother is a Jewish disciple of Jesus. In 2 Timothy 1:5, we learn her name is Eunice and her mother, Lois, Timothy's grandmother, is also a disciple. It is these two women who bring up the young pastor and teach him about Jesus. They are wonderful models to encourage women to raise their children in the faith. Paul commends Timothy on his great faith, which he attributes to Grandma Lois and Mama Eunice:

> "I am reminded of your sincere faith, which first lived in

your grandmother Lois and in your mother Eunice and, I am persuaded, now lives in you also." — 2 Timothy 1:5

Then there is Priscilla who Paul calls his "co-worker" (Romans 16:3-4). And let us not forget the rich businesswoman, Lydia of Thyatira (Acts 16:14-15), who is considered the first European convert and a purveyor of purple, a highly desired and expensive fabric.

Also in Romans 16:1-2, Paul mentions Phoebe who is a deacon in the church at Cenchreae. She is trusted to deliver Paul's epistle to the Roman church and Paul calls her a benefactor. There is also Nympha (Colossians 4:15) who has a house church in Laodicea where she serves as the pastor. Scholars believe that Nympha is also the "dear lady" that John refers to in 2 John 1:5:

> "...And now, dear lady, I am not writing you a new command but one we have had from the beginning. I ask that we love one another. And this is love: that we walk in obedience to his commands. As you have heard from the beginning, his command is that you walk in love." — 2 John 1:4-5

From these home churches, thousands of women go into the world, preaching and declaring the Good News, and their number grows to millions. Throughout the New Testament, women disciples play a major role in evangelizing, leading churches, providing funds and serving as role models in the Christian community.

Their contribution to the early church is more than significant. Women's lives are transformed by their encounter with the Son of God. As John 8:36 says, "So if the Son sets you free, you will be free indeed!"

As one final note, I'd like you to take heart to what our Savior says in John 13:34-35 about what is expected of a disciple of Jesus:

"A new command I give you: Love one another. As I have loved you, so you must love one another. By this everyone will know that you are my disciples, if you love one another."

~ ~ ~ ~ ~

MEDITATION

God chose you. You are not an accident. Your life was created to glorify him. He gave you talents, gifts, intelligence, spiritual awareness and much more. You are a follower of Jesus and so you are one of his disciples.

Meditate on the gifts you have and ask the Lord to show you how to serve him with these gifts. You do not need to be afraid of what he will ask you to do because he knows your heart. He will be with you always.

...for God's gifts and his call are irrevocable. — Romans 11:29

Then Jesus came to them and said, 'All authority in heaven and on earth has been given to me. Therefore go and make disciples of all nations, baptizing them in the name of the Father and of the Son and of the Holy Spirit, and teaching them to obey everything I have commanded you. And surely I am with you always, to the very end of the age.' — Matthew 28:18-20

Study Guide Questions

WOMEN DISCIPLES

— List three things you want to remember about each of the women disciples.

— Do you identify with one of the women disciples more than the others? Which one? Why?

— Are you surprised to learn there are women disciples? How does this change the way you look at your ministry or service to God?

— Why is Romans 16:7 important for women who are called to leadership in the church? What can you do to support Christian women leaders?

— Now that you see women served in multiple capacities with Jesus, does it free you to serve him as you are called? What does it mean to be his disciple?

— Have you received a call for works of service, intercessory prayer, pastoring, teaching or evangelism? What prevents you? Can you now make a commitment to follow Christ as he has called you? What steps do you need to take to move forward?

NOTES

ENDNOTES

INTRODUCTION

[1] *Shekinah* in Hebrew means "the dwelling." It is the presence or manifestation of God who "dwells" among (Old Testament) or within (New Testament) us. It represents the Holy Spirit or Glory of God and since it is a feminine word has come to represent the feminine attributes of God as manifested by the Holy Spirit—or the Comforter.

In the New Testament—since there is no Greek equivalent—Shekinah means radiance, or light or glory as in Second Corinthians 4:6, "For God, who said, 'Let light shine out of darkness,' made his light shine in our hearts to give us the light of the knowledge of God's glory displayed in the face of Christ." Shekinah has also been characterized as being represented by a "dove" since Shekinah has "wings."

Jewish Encyclopedia. 2012. Web. Retrieved August, 2012 from Jewish Encyclopedia.com/articles/13437-shekinah.

[2] Barna Research. "Christian Women Today, Part 1 of 4: What Women Think of Faith, Leadership and Their Role in the Church," August 13, 2012. Web. Retrieved from www.barna.org/research releases/culture & media

[3] Pew Research Center. "America's Changing Religious Landscape," 2015. Web. Retrieved 2015 from www.pewforum.org.

I - MOTHER MARY: THE EARLY YEARS

[4] Scholars often disagree on the genealogy of Mary. However, there is a possibility Mary married Joseph because they were both of the tribe of Judah. Numbers 36:1-13 shows how this is possible. Zelophehad's daughters complain to Moses that because their father had no sons they would lose their inheritance. Moses sought the Lord and answered them in verses 6-7, which state: "This is what the Lord commands for Zelophehad's daughters: They may marry anyone they please as long as they marry within their father's tribal clan. No inheritance in Israel is to pass from one tribe to another, for every Israelite shall keep the tribal inheritance of their ancestors." There is a possibility Mary married into her own tribe, which supports the claim she is of the line of David. It also may explain the differences between Luke's and Matthew's genealogies.

IV - PROPHET ANNA

[5] Reid, Barbara. *Choosing The Better Part?* Order of St. Benedict. Liturgical Press, 1996: 90. Print.

[6] Getty-Sullivan, Mary Ann. *Women in the New Testament.* The Liturgical Press. Collegeville, Minnesota. 2001: 38. Print.

[7] Fairchild, Mary. "Bible Numerology: The Meaning of Numbers in the Bible," About Religion, 2009. Web. Retrieved 2015 from christianity. about.com/od/biblefactsandlists/qt/Bible-Numerology.htm.

[8] Luke refers to widows more often than any other Gospel writer. For more in depth study, read Luke 7:11-17, 18:1-8, 20:47, as well as Mark 12:41-44, Acts 6:1-6, 9:36-43.

VI - BLEEDING WOMAN

[9] Diamant, Anita. *The Red Tent*. St. Martin's Press, 1997. Print.

VII - CRIPPLED WOMAN

[10] National Osteoporosis Foundation. Web. Retrieved 2015 from www. nof.org.

[11] Ibid.

X - CANAANITE WOMAN

[12] Strong LL.D., S.T.D., James. *Strong's Dictionary of the Bible, Greek and Hebrew*, 1890. Print.

[13] Skirbekk, Gunnar and Gilje, Nils, *A History of Western Thought: From Ancient Greece to the Twentieth Century*, Routledge, 2001: 80. Print.

[14] Strong LL.D., S.T.D., James. *Strong's Dictionary of the Bible, Greek and Hebrew*, 1890. Print.

[15] *Mirriam-Webster Dictionary*. Mirriam-Webster, Inc, 2016. Print.

[16] *John Wesley's Commentary on the Bible*. Zondervan. Abridged edition, 1990. Print.

[17] Gench, Frances Taylor. *Back to the Well*. Westminster John Knox Press. Kentucky, 2004: 21. Print.

XI - SAMARITAN WOMAN

[18] Edersheim, Alfred. *The Life and Times of Jesus the Messiah*. 2012. vol. i. Book III, ch. viii, Appendix XV. Print.

[19] Orr, James, M.A., D.D. General Editor. "Jacob's Well." *International Standard Bible Encyclopedia*, 1915. Web. Retrieved 2015 from www.studylight.org.

[20] Encyclopedia Britannica, Inc. "Mount Gerizim," Web. Retrieved 2012 from www.britannica.com.

XII - SISTERS: MARTHA AND MARY

[21] Strong LL.D., S.T.D., James. *Strong's Dictionary of the Bible, Greek and Hebrew*, 1890. Print.

XIII - ANOINTING WOMAN

[22] Bourgeault, Cynthia, *The Meaning of Mary Magdalene*. Shambhala. Boston, 2010: 22. Print.

[23] Oils and Plants, Spikenard. Web. Retrieved 2015 from www.oilsandplants.com/spikenard

XIV - WANTON WOMAN

[24] Clarke, Adam. "Adam Clarke's Bible Commentary," John 8, verse 3. Web. Retrieved from www.godrules.net/library/clarke/clarkejoh8.htm.

[25] Chumney, Edward. "The Seven Festivals of the Messiah." Treasure House, Shippensburg, PA, 2001: 5. (Zechariah 14:16).

[26] Gench, Frances Taylor. *Back to the Well*. Westminster John Knox Press. Kentucky, 2004:137. Print.

XV - MARY MAGDALENE

[27] Merk, A. (1910). Magdala. "The Catholic Encyclopedia". New York: Robert Appleton Company. Web. Retrieved 2012 from New Advent: http://www.newadvent.org/cathen/09523a.htm.

[28] Leclercq, H. (1911). "The First Council of Nicaea," The Catholic Encyclopedia. New York: Robert Appleton Company. Web. Retrieved August 6, 2012 from New Advent: www.newadvent.org/cathen/11044a.htm.

[29] Meyer, Marvin, ed. with De Boer, Esther A. *The Gospels of Mary: The Secret Tradition of Mary Magdalene the Companion of Jesus*. Harper. San Francisco, 2004. Print.

[30] Owens MD, Lance. The Gnostic Society Library. The Nag Hammadi Library Introduction. Web. Retrieved 2015 from www.gnosis.org.

[31] King, Karen L. *The Gospel of Mary of Magdala: Jesus and the First Woman Apostle*. Polebridge Press, Santa Rosa, California, 2003: 3-12. Print.

[32] Owens MD, Lance. The Gnostic Society Library. The Nag Hammadi Library, Introduction. Web. Retrieved 2015 from www.gnosis.org.

[33] Meyer, Marvin with De Boer, Esther A., *The Gospels of Mary.* Harper. San Francisco, 2004: 35. Print.

[34] The Relics of Saint Marie-Magdalene at La Sainte Baume, Diocese of Frejus-Toulon, Southern France, provided by Eternal Word Television Network. Translated from the French by Deacon E. Scott Borgman. Web. Retrieved 2015 from www.ewtn.com/library/CHISTORY/relicsmarmagdal

[35] The Nazarene Way of Essenic Studies. "The Legends of Mary Magdalene". Web. Retrieved 2015 from www.thenazareneway.com/life_of_st_mary_magdalene.htm

XVI - WOMEN DISCIPLES

[36] Jesus sent his disciples out two-by-two for a reason. His action recalls the story of Noah in which two of every kind, male and female, went into the ark to be saved? However, in this case, two went out together, male and female, from the true "Ark" [Jesus] to save the world.

[37] Bauckham, Richard. *Gospel Women: Studies of the Named Women in the Gospels.* William B. Eerdmans Publishing Company. Grand Rapids, Michigan, 2002:121-134. Print.

[38] Ibid, 137.

[39] Ibid, 165.

[40] Ibid, 205-208.

SUGGESTED READING

Bauckham, Richard. *Gospel Women: Studies of the Named Women in the Gospels*. William B. Eerdmans Publishing Company. Grand Rapids, Michigan. 2002.

Bourgeault, Cynthia. *The Meaning of Mary Magdalene: Discovering the Woman at the Heart of Christianity*. Shambhala, Boston, 2010.

Gench, Frances Taylor. *Back to the Well: Women's Encounters with Jesus in the Gospels*. Westminster John Knox Press. Louisville, Kentucky, 2004.

Getty-Sullivan, Mary Ann. *Women in the New Testament.* The Liturgical Press. Collegeville, Minnesota, 2001.

Grady, J. Lee. *10 Lies the Church Tells Women: How the Bible Has Been Misused to Keep Women in Spiritual Bondage*. Charisma House, Strang Communications Company. Lake Mary, Florida, 2000.

Meyer, Marvin & De Boer, Esther A. *The Gospels of Mary: The Secret Tradition of Mary Magdalene, The Companion of Jesus*. Harper Collins, 2004.

Mickelsen, Alvera, editor. *Women, Authority & the Bible.* InterVarsity Press. Downers Grove, Illinois, 1986

Reid, Barbara. *Choosing the Better Part? Women in the Gospel of Luke*. A Michael Glazier Book. The Liturgical Press, Collegeville, Minnesota, 1996.

Sumner, Ph.D., Sarah. *Men and Women in the Church: Building Consensus on Christian Leadership.* InterVarsity Press. Downers Grove, Illinois, 2003.

ABOUT THE AUTHOR

Deborah Kaine Thompson began life on the shores of Maryland but grew up on the desert plains of southeast Idaho where she started writing. In 1971 she became a follower of Christ at the height of the 'Jesus Movement' and began writing to spread the gospel and encourage and empower women as disciples.

After taking a master's degree in writing from California State University, Northridge, she worked as a reporter for two California newspapers. She later established a career in higher education as a communications professional.

She is the author of several books, including a memoir on her covert trip into Romania during the Cold War titled *Perilous Journey: The Memoir of a Bible Smuggler*. Her two works of Christian fiction are *When Gods Collide* and *The Living Stones*.

Today, when not writing, she works as an editor for E-maginative Writing, provides writing workshops and speaks at academic and literary venues.

The mother of two adult sons lives in Mesa, Arizona.

~ ~ ~ ~ ~

59850277R00163

Made in the USA
San Bernardino, CA
08 December 2017